EVERYONE HAS A STORY OR TWO

A collection of memories from inspired older
people as part of our writing challenges.

Age UK Richmond upon Thames
www.ageukrichmond.org.uk

EVERYONE HAS A STORY OR TWO
A collection of memories from the Age UK Richmond
writing challenge.

ISBN: 978-1-0369-0474-6

Disclaimer
The opinions, beliefs and viewpoints expressed belong to the individual contributors and do not necessarily reflect those of Age UK Richmond. The content is not intended to offend in any way.

Cover by Natalie Pattenden
Design by Natalie Pattenden
Printed by Minuteman Press Hampton Hill

Please donate to us. Your kind support will fuel projects like this one, which contribute to older people in Richmond upon Thames living healthier, happier more independent later lives.
Visit our website www.ageukrichmond.org.uk

Age UK Richmond upon Thames is a registered charity and company limited by guarantee.
Registered in England and Wales number 4116911. Registered charity number 1084211.
Registered office: The White House Community Centre, 45 The Avenue, Hampton, Richmond upon Thames, TW12 3RN.

FOREWORD

Age UK Richmond published our first Everyone Has a Story book in 2021. We had an excellent response, both from those who wrote about their memorable moments and from those who enjoyed reading them. We knew that there were plenty more tales to tell. We are so pleased to bring together more stories for this new collection. It has been a pleasure to once again celebrate the lives of older people in Richmond upon Thames. Initiatives like this enable people to preserve their legacy and share their wisdom with future generations. I am grateful to our enthusiastic staff who have worked on this project as well as to all those who have taken the time to write.

We hope you enjoy reading their stories.

Gavin Shand

Chief Executive
Age UK Richmond

A word from Marie-Therese Keegan, Wellbeing Services Coordinator and Writing Challenge project lead.

A memorable moment can take you far. It took our contributors to Paris, Africa, Hong Kong, Japan, Australia and beyond. To new ventures, school days, a wedding day, war and atonement. Stories that were passed down are shared with us. We are given nuggets of wisdom gleaned over time.

What started out as a writing challenge once again has delivered us a book. We were delighted that broadcaster and journalist Angela Rippon CBE and St Mary's University Lecturer (Creative Writing) Dr Russell Schechter agreed to be our judges and choose their favourites. We had a couple of Age UK Richmond reader awards too.

We hope you will enjoy these stories and may even feel inspired to write down your own memorable moments.

"The man who writes about himself and his own time is the only man who writes about all people and about all time."
George Bernard Shaw

CONTENTS

ACKNOWLEDGEMENTS

We would like to thank all the people who took the time to write their stories and share their memories with us.

With gratitude also to our editorial and production team – Marie-Therese Keegan, Aydee Burke, Natalie Pattenden and our judges – Angela Rippon CBE and Dr Russell Schechter.

Thank you to our prize sponsors

Arts Society Richmond
The Petersham Hotel
Tactical Employment Solicitors
Ham House and Garden
Turner's House

Finding Love
Jean Dowse, 90

Angela Rippon's Choice Award ⭐

Love is being fourteen and in love. We have just finished a game of football, three girls and eight boys, and I am walking home with George. He is eighteen, the 'idol' of the gang, and he has asked me to be his girlfriend, oh joy! My father is not pleased, too old he thinks. Can I go to Wembley to see the Speedway? Only if I am in by 9.45.

Two years have gone by, I am still in love, we are still together. In another two years we are engaged and will be married within eighteen months.

I am a mother at twenty, looking at my baby daughter, and now I know what love is. Eighteen months later I have another little one to love, Andrew. He is the sweetest baby and my heart overflows. I feel very rich and there will be another baby in two years' time. Three little people to love.

Unfortunately, although I have all this love to give, my first love, my husband, has too much love and shares it with someone else, of which I am unaware.

As the years go on, marriage becomes stale, and love departs. It is then that I meet the love of my life. Eventually we are married, and I find out the true meaning of love. Love is not just passion; it is friendship and letting go to enable yourselves to pursue your own interests. The years pass by unnoticed; you are happy to-gether and suddenly not young anymore, but this doesn't mean you are no longer in love, just a different comfortable love.

Suddenly disaster strikes. A disabling stroke for him. Now that love is stretched to its limits. Your friend and partner has formed a new personality, you are living with someone you don't quite know, but it is not their fault. Frustration overpowers them at times. You must prove your love for them. You have to. Wash, dress, feed and care for them, and remember all the good days that went before and take advantage of the good days to come even though they might be few. And when they are no longer here you still love them for making your life so wonderful.

View From The Top
Janet Teal Daniel

I look down from the window of the second-floor apartment onto the view below. To the left is a children's fun fair, a merry-go-round of cartoon animals and the sound of children laughing. A few motor cyclists are sitting on their bikes chatting, their black leather jackets glistening in the early morning sunshine. I notice the tide is way out leaving a long stretch of wet sand and a few cold-water swimmers shivering as they stumble up the beach to Marco's café.

It's Barry Island. June 1st 2024. We are in Barry for the Festival of the Sea, and Wales first Sea Shanty Festival. The event is held to celebrate and raise funds for the RNLI 200th anniversary. The Royal National Lifeboat Institution.

Barry was immortalised in the BBC comedy series, Gavin & Stacey, running from 2007. The last Christmas Day special in 2019 had 18.49 million viewers in the UK, the most-watched comedy in 17 years. The story, written by Ruth Jones and James

Corden, revolves around the long-distance relationship between Gavin from Billericay in Essex and Stacey from Barry, Vale of Glamorgan, South Wales and their families.

I look down at the view again. It's the 25th of July 1979 and there we are, Janet from Battersea and Rhys from Pontypridd. We'd just met on a photography course in the Barry Summer School, an annual two week residential, offering adult courses across the range of arts and music. It was famous for the performers and teachers it attracted. It had an international reputation for jazz. It also had a reputation for students arriving with one partner and leaving with another.

I blinked. We weren't actually there by the merry-go-round or sitting having coffee at Marco's. We were supposed to be there. I was social secretary and had organised a trip to the fairground. In the spirit of the residential, we were somewhere else up the coast, enjoying a bacon buttie and sharing stories of our individual travels and adventures in Argentina, Greece, Indonesia and elsewhere. I shifted again. I heard Rhys humming the tune of the sea shanty Keep Haulin' as he went into the bathroom. I joined in, and like what often happens, a hum becomes a voice.Then two.

After breakfast we sauntered up the promenade past the Big Dipper and Ghost Train and saw a group of people standing around a red marquee. We pushed forward and peeped in. The blue blazered Barry Male Voice Choir was coming to the end of a moving harmony about Gwalia Wales.

Sea shanties date back to the 16th century but really flourished during the 19th century on board large merchant sailing ships.

Square-rigged vessels like Cutty Sark required groups of men to coordinate in winding and hauling ropes and setting the sails for long exhausting periods.

Wales has no tradition of singing sea shanties, but some men from South Wales decided to change all that and Bois Y Bryn / Boys from the Hill was formed. They invited groups from Devon and Cornwall to perform in this first ever Welsh sea shanty festival. The male voice choir ended with Wellerman, a whaling song popularised in 2021 by Scottish Postman, Nathan Evans, who became an overnight star when he posted his version on social media, and it went viral.

'Call and response' is a form of music that has roots in Africa. Here, one person sings a line of a song, and this is repeated by the rest of the group. We responded to the call of the lead singer with gusto and vigour, showing our throats to one another like hungry seagulls. As Barry's choir finished, some people moved away from the marquee, and we moved in to grab a pallet stool near the front to enjoy the day's entertainment. The groups with names like Shantyjacs, Severn Whalers, The Rusty Tubs, Barnacle Buoys were mainly made up of men, some dressed as pirates or sailors. There were a few exceptions of all women groups, such as Drecklys, a group of 12 acapella singers. The Cornish leader said that Drecklys meant something like Manyana, but more so! They told the stories of the women left behind when the men went off to sea.

We fed our throats with pints of lager and fish and chips and at the end of the evening staggered back to our digs, Wellerman'd out. It was in the repertoire of almost every group. We must have sung the song all through six or seven times.

The June sun is setting over Barry Island. I look down again and see among a future crowd, two much older people, hand in hand, softly singing, 'Hold your course and don't let go. Keep haulin' boys'.

Almost Out Of Fuel

Hazell Jacobs, 91

Who would have imagined running short of fuel might lead to such an extraordinary encounter? The prospect of being stranded in a rental car on a dusty desert road mile from anywhere was alarming.

I had left San Francisco, my temporary adopted home, to rendezvous in Albuquerque with my husband who was working in Texas. Our destination was Santa Fe in New Mexico, a vibrant city of culture, associated with Georgia O'Keefe, D.H.Lawrence, colourful art and crafts and above all, native Indian history and its present-day recognition. Flights were on time; we rented a car and after an uneventful journey we reached our destination. The weekend passed all too quickly. Suddenly it was Sunday morning, and we faced the long car journey back to catch our planes. We then realised we had used up all our gas on a side trip to Taos. No problem, we thought. This is the USA...plenty of gas stations in

Santa Fe. Wrong! Unfamiliar with the area, we were now heading West, city behind and that darned needle was showing EMPTY! The desert, with all these rattlesnakes and miles of empty road, was not inviting. We turned off the freeway and landed lucky...a tiny gas station. Relieved, I consulted my guidebook and discovered on that particular day there was the Green Corn Festival in the Santo Domingo Indian Pueblo nearby.

We parked in a rough car park with very old battered trucks and cars, looked at the crudely written signs...NO LIQUOR... NO PHOTOS, and tentatively walked in. We were the only white faces there and felt like intruders. That was soon forgotten as we witnessed the most remarkable spectacle in all our years in the USA. I was in my element looking at stalls selling blankets, pottery, beaded objects, silver and turquoise jewellery. I was admiring beaded earrings made by a beautiful woman named Shadow who had one child clinging to her skirt, another nursing at her breast. The next stall holder, her husband, was selling music cassettes. Hearing my accent, he asked where I was from. I assumed they were native Indians by their dress and suntanned skins. Now comes the big surprise!

He handed me a card advertising his music. It read "James Lascelles". Not a surname one expects at a festival begging the gods to bless the green corn to ensure a good harvest later. I told him I had met someone with the same name "Lascelles" in England many years before. I didn't think an American Indian would be interested in my story of The British Racing Drivers Ball in Windsor, and the unexpected invitation for a nightcap at Fort Belvedere from its President, the Honourable Gerald Lascelles,

8

first cousin to the late Queen Elizabeth.....or how gob smacked I had felt sitting in the chair where Edward the Eighth had broadcast his Abdication. I don't usually mix in aristocratic circles, but it was my husband's love of motor racing which led to meeting Graham Hill, Grand Prix champion and the Queen's cousin Gerald at that ball. I was stunned when the long haired, tanned man wearing a colourful bandana round his head quietly said "Gerald Lascelles is my uncle". This man before me was the Queen's cousin, once removed! He wanted to know what I was doing at the festival. I explained our desire to visit Santa Fe before we finally returned to London, running out of gas, etc. In this day of surprises, it turned out that his birthplace as son to Marion Stein, the pianist and the Earl of Harewood, was Orme Court, Bayswater, a few hundred yards from our London home!

I was so amazed I hardly thanked my husband for the beautiful silver necklace, carved as two feathers holding a turquoise stone, secretly bought whilst I chatted.

But now the excitement within the crowd was rising. We left the stalls trying to look inconspicuous and made our way towards the low sweat lodge where the chief and his male followers had held their private meeting. The drumming was pounding as they emerged, wearing magnificent feathered headdresses and gleaming silver and turquoise jewellery. They danced wildly so their gods might bless the green corn. We were now hemmed in by crowds and the heat was intense. Our escape? The rental car? Our flights? The gods were kind to us.

The Spanish gave the name of Santo Domingo to the pueblo, but in 2009 the local people changed it back to the Indian name of Kewa. Today, James is still playing music with the group TALK-ING SPIRITS. The child Shadow was nursing, Tewa, now 39, plays in a progressive punk band. His beautiful mother died very young and my beloved husband died twenty years ago.

Each time I wear the silver and turquoise necklace, I fondly remember.

Adventures

Sarina de Majo, 70

Somehow, I have managed to survive with only the memory of sitting near the mudflats watching the water twinkling in the sun and listening to the sound of curlews calling. It has been nearly twenty years since I have visited the estuary.

There have been times when I thought without actually being there in person, the liquid healing would disappear, but today, with light soft rain falling on the skylight above me, with a warm and dozing dog beside me, I can recall the estuary with enough conviction to feel the change it always brought to my frame of mind.

That strangely comforting smell of slightly sewage-polluted water, the sheep grazing on the marsh and the sight of the little island just far enough offshore to have been a forbidden place. The currents in the water where the river meets the sea are notorious.

I think each of us had a near death experience resulting from listening to warnings but not heeding them.

Once I climbed down into the water with my young cousin and her friend and realised after just a few minutes that I remained stationary in spite of making what I thought were measured and strong strokes with my arms.

I remember a strange sense of calm settling on me as I realised I could neither turn towards the bank nor make headway towards a large rock which might have offered respite.

That day, unusually, a fisherman was sitting nearby, and realising we were in trouble, he leaned in and helped us out.

The shivering and chattering of our teeth was overpowered by the promises we made each other to keep the adventure a secret from my aunt and grandmother, both of whom reminded us frequently of the dangers of swimming in the estuary at anything other than slack tide.

Slack tide in this place meant miles of clean rippled sand criss-crossed by shallow glittering channels. The space around you when you were in the middle of the emptied bay was so wonderful. The Welsh hills on three sides playing hide and seek with the clouds, and in the far distance a just visible lick of light on the real sea.

Shells and firm sand and softer sand underfoot and birds everywhere. Stiff legged waders and curlews, little gulls running with clockwork steps, feeding on the shrimps quivering in the remains of the sea, crows and sea-gulls wheeling over the small cliffs, and the occasional hawk hovering high above us all.

"The tide comes in faster than a galloping horse" we were told.

If you notice the channels which barely cover your feet beginning to fill, then is the time to take yourself to the edge of the sand and scramble up to safety.

The ribbons of water had a confusing and ever-changing system of ebb and flow, and it was easy to find yourself surrounded by sudden deep and fast flowing troughs which were difficult to negotiate.

When I was a teenager, I had a friend to stay. We went for a walk and a smoke on the sands and were taken by surprise by the tide's turn. Within minutes we were trapped in a cat's cradle of intersecting channels. J could not swim.

The calm which comes when I realise I am in extreme danger, descended, and apparently unconcerned, I tied our clothes into a bundle which I placed on my head, and taking J by the hand, I dragged us both through current filled channels, at first ankle and then chest deep. We reached the bank and I pushed J up the rough grass to safety just before we were out of our depth in the swirling brown water.

There was one farm on the island, and we walked up the hill with trembling legs and asked to use their telephone to ring my grandmother to tell her we were safe.

My friend resumed contact thirty years later and came to have supper.

'You saved my life' she said. Until reminded, I had forgotten the entire event, but I'm glad we didn't drown that day.

What I haven't forgotten is the excitement and relief I felt every time I returned to that estuary.

I would sit on the familiar outcrop inhaling the smell of the marshy land, watching it being grazed by the handful of sheep, listening to the welcome sound of the curlews calling in the evening sun, and feel my spirits rise and settle.

A Trip to Greece in 1958

George Roussopoulos

It was in 1958 that I hitchhiked to Greece for what was my first independent visit to Greece. I met three school friends in Athens - Socrates, Andrew and Philip, and we hired a car for a gloriously mad week. We left for Delphi but after 30km the car slowed to a snail's pace and then stopped! The clutch was worn out but fortunately a local garage fixed it.

Our next target was Patras to the south, then Olympia. In the mountains we heard of a 'panigiri' that night in a small village. It is an annual feast commemorating the saint day of its church. It must have been the 15th August and the Feast of the Virgin and we were the only strangers.

A space by the church and a fire roasting a lamb, ancient stone benches, a table covered in mounds of meat and bread … and rivers of retsina, the traditional Greek wine which is resinated to preserve it in a hot climate when fridges had not been invented.

Songs and dances through the night - the Tsamikos, Kalama-tianos, Syrtos - to the accompaniment of a few bouzouki (an instrument resembling a guitar) and flutes.

A long night. I got up the next morning on a muddy patch in a field where I must have drifted unconsciously, overcome by the wine. Ah, they don't do them like that everywhere anymore ... but they are still worth a big detour.

We then decided to tackle Mount Olympus, the highest mountain in Greece at 2,917m, better known as the home of the Gods.

A train took us to its foot at Litochoro and the trek started from almost sea level. We did not have a good map, soon lost the trail and elected to follow a stream. As it rose it grew wilder and wilder, steepened. Andrew, in front of me, stepped over an adder; a few minutes later it was Philip. In a panic we left the stream and scrambled up the dangerous crags. Hours later, exhausted, weary, scratched and bitten, we ran across a path and reached the monastery of Ayios Dyonisios. The hospitable monks fed and found beds for us, and the next morning we set out again for the heights.

When night fell, we came across some shepherds who had built a fire. They generously shared their bread and cheese with us. It was bitterly cold, and we all slept around the fire. At 2 o'clock in the morning we were woken by thunder and lightning and a del-uge of rain. Still half awake, we grabbed our bags, all adjourned to a cave nearby and quickly fell asleep again. As time passed, it got warmer and warmer, more and more comfortable. The fol-lowing morning, we found out why: the sheep had followed us into the cave and covered us!

Saying goodbye to the shepherds we set off again for the top.

After a few hours we were astonished to find half a dozen shelters resembling wigwams and built of woven branches. In front of them, a few women spinning wool. They were ashen blond and very beautiful; spoke a language we did not recognize. There were no men - they were out with the sheep further up the mountain. Later I found out they were Sarakatsani, an ancient nomadic people who were scattered through the Greek highlands. Today they have almost vanished as they were more or less forcibly resettled in villages and towns - a museum in Serres is devoted to them.

Near the peak we were overtaken by three young Germans.

"Where have you come from?" we asked.

"From Litochoro"

"And when did you leave?"

"This morning, and we shall be back there tonight."

Our pride at our achievement suddenly vanished: in one day they would accomplish what had taken us three days! Still, we have our memories of the shepherds and the sheep and the snakes and the Sarakatsani, well worth the extra time.

Whisky Echo
Joseph F Ryan, 68

Dr Russell Schechter's Choice Award ⭐

I walked up Onslow Road to meet my father after his shift and see if he could help me make sense of my experience. My Dad, Paddy Ryan, worked as a nursing orderly on Richmond Hill, at the Royal Star & Garter Home for disabled ex-services personnel, for over 40 years. In his time, he helped hundreds of people, including a handful who had been awarded Britain's highest military decoration for valour: the Victoria Cross. Paddy was often nursing and supporting people at the end of their lives. He was, therefore, familiar with death. So was my mother, Dorothy, who worked as a nurse in India during the Second World War, including during the bombing of Kolkata (Calcutta).

Despite attempts by my parents to shield me from life's shocks, every child eventually suffers a wounding. As a 12-year-old schoolboy, I would travel home from Chertsey to Richmond by train. On Monday 8 April 1968, I stepped down onto the platform at Staines in order to find a less crowded carriage. As I did so, I glanced upwards and saw an aeroplane leaving a trail of raging fire.

BOAC Flight 712 was a Boeing 707-465, call sign Whisky Echo, ultimately bound for Sydney. On take-off at 4.27 pm, it suffered an engine failure, which quickly led to a major blaze. The plane was ordered to bank to the left and return to Heathrow Airport. From my vantage point, I saw an engine on the port wing break away and fall over the village of Thorpe. The aircraft continued its turn and dropped lower as it approached the aerodrome. For one moment, as it descended, it looked as if it might crash onto the stationary train. Instead, the aircraft roared past overhead, and the pilot managed to make a good landing, despite the potentially destabilising loss of one engine. Unfortunately, there was still about 22,000 gallons of fuel in the plane and a series of explosions sent columns of filthy black smoke into the sky.

From 127 people onboard, five people died and over 30 were injured, yet 122 escaped with their lives. John Davis, the air traffic controller who assisted the flight, was awarded an MBE. Among the crew, the Chief Steward, Neville Davis-Gordon, calmly but firmly directed passengers to available exits and was awarded a British Empire Medal for Gallantry. Stewardess Jane Harrison was awarded a posthumous George Cross, the highest award possible for a civilian, for her bravery in trying to save the lives of others. She was observed standing in one of the plane's exits, ready to slide down an escape chute to safety. Jane, however, must have realised that there were still four passengers left inside, including an eight-year-old girl and a disabled person unable to move unaided. In what Anthony Crosland, MP, called a 'lonely and courageous action', she was last seen turning back into the inferno of the stricken plane. Jane was one of only four women to have been awarded the George Cross for heroism, the other three (Odette Sansom, Violette Szabo and Noor Inayat Khan) being recipients for their resistance work with the Special Operations Executive in Nazi-occupied France during World War II.

At the time of the Whisky Echo disaster, I feared the lethal force of the falling engine and stood transfixed as it tumbled earthwards but learnt later that it plunged safely into a gravel pit. For some moments, I was horrified by the imminent prospect of the plane crashing onto the railway station and incinerating everyone in a gigantic fireball. As the thick coils of smoke rose high into the sky, however, I was left with the ghastly realisation that sudden death must have claimed some, or maybe all, on the aeroplane. It was a sombre moment, a time to hope for a miracle. It was also the time when my childhood innocence ended. I have not needed the passage of over half a century to realise deeply the lesson that death comes to us all. Sir Winston Churchill, familiar with danger himself, wrote: 'Courage is rightly esteemed the first of human qualities, because ... it is the quality which guarantees all others.' Jane Harrison, at just 22 years old, showed such fortitude, determination and courage that she remains inspirational. May we all demonstrate a similar courage facing illness, disability, old age and death. On reflection, however, there was another lesson to be learned: live each moment mindfully, with wonder and gratitude, and keep words in your heart that eternally sing out: 'Thank you, thank you!'

When I was twelve

When I was twelve,
we had so much fun.
We played make believe,
chase & run

When I was twelve,
I grew up fast, no longer
a boy, a man with a past

When I was twelve, I saw
you fall, unable to help,
cannot save them all

Now I am old, I look back
now, save the boy, I sigh
with furrowed brow.

Now I can play, and laugh
once more, because I know
the boy lives, forever more.

Poem and Drawing by
Genevieve Hollis, Joseph's daughter.

21

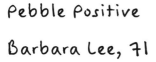

Pebble Positive

Barbara Lee, 71

I was 71 on August 14th. Age has not defined my life, but time has. I met my friend Maryline at school when we were both 12 years old. We both love to write, and now I go down to Eastbourne, and we watch the sea, and the pebbles and we inspire each other with our stories and poetry, and she is helping me put together ideas for the poetry and writing groups I now run.

I had a secret dream when I was a child, that one day I would be a writer or a teacher and be clever like the others. But sadly I failed my 11 plus, and didn't pass exams at school. I was very disappointed with myself. I drifted from job to job as a secretary, and then when I got to 22, I wanted to be educated and clever, so I went to night school for two years to get my A levels. I remember going out in the snow and freezing cold on the bus to college to give in an assignment and I never missed a class. When I got my English and Sociology, I didn't believe it was me, but someone else, and I thought what do I do with this now? I got into the University of Westminster to do a Social Science Degree, but I didn't have Maths. And I was fine with writing and researching, but then I did a module in Statistics, and had a panic attack and my mind went blank, and I got zero. But I didn't give up. And with college support I passed next time round.

It took me five years to do my part time degree course. It was the moment that changed my life forever, but I would have to wait many years more to know what a life changing moment it was. The day I got my degree I was pregnant with my first child. That smiling photo of me with my degree hat and certificate looks at me from the mantelpiece every day to remind me of what I achieved.

But I had another role to play, with a young family I was soon to be a single parent. I needed to earn an income, I needed to train to be someone, and so more studying followed, and in between bringing up my children, I qualified as an adult education teacher. An opportunity came to work part-time at a college. Then at age 49 I started applying for a full-time role. I went for three interviews, each time I was higher on the list. At the third attempt, just after my 50th birthday, I started my first ever full-time post as a teacher in an adult education college. More studying followed, including a diploma in my chosen field of English as an additional language.

My career in full time education ended when I was 60. Ten amazing years with my own team, my own office, meetings, lesson plans, and an opportunity that I took to teach in China during two summer holiday months.

At 60, after ten intense rewarding years, my time as a full-time teacher ended, I was able to start on new journeys. In 2012 I was selected to be a games maker in the London Olympics, volunteering at the Commonwealth Games, and a summer warden at Buckingham Palace. Then I was offered some teaching in Spain, and the world really did become my Oyster.

But what about my other dream of writing? I got my degree because I was able to articulate things I thought about down on paper. I was a secret writer, I wrote letters to friends, and did school projects. And wrote poetry.

Then the pandemic came, my outside world shut down, I got shingles, covid, and I had a major fall where I broke my wrist. But in that small space at home, I began to write poems. I was asked to read some out on Zoom. And then I was asked to teach on Zoom.

Last year I was asked to be part of the community actors on the stage at Richmond Theatre, and to hear the audience applauding, and to be dressed up and be someone else for a week, was just an amazing experience for me.

Now through my poetry and writing workshops, I feel I can give something to others, of my dreams that I had all those years ago. And I will go and watch the sea and and my friend and I will go on with our stories and poems always Pebble Positive.

Boat

Victoria Johnson, 58

I am like a small boat in a big ocean. Floating...just.

The water, at present, is calm. I am grateful for the peace and so I grab the opportunity to stop and breathe. I survey my surroundings. All seems ok; nothing has changed, nothing is out of place. I then wonder how long it will be before the next hiccup, or storm, or wave comes crashing down on top of me.

Hush. Enjoy the calm Vicki.

It doesn't take long before another link in the 'chain' has been added. The chain that is attached to the heavy anchor that keeps me from drifting away, from moving, and from leaving. The 'anchor' is my family. The 'links' in the chain are the issues and the problems that come with my family - ill health, dependency, commitments, wrong choices, finances, love. There is an additional health worry this time. More emails and meetings now need to be done, and another nibble of time gets eaten away from my days ahead. This chain gets longer and the anchor gets heavier.

My boat... I ... will be stuck here; tied down for a long while yet.

When it's quiet I really should use the time usefully. Take stock. Catch up. Tidy; tidy my surroundings, and my head. Regulate - sleep, eating, and breathing... all three I struggle with. Sleeping far too little is not good for the head. Eating only when there is time and not when I need it to refuel the body. Breathing, so normal, but I am known to fret and worry ... not good for the heart or soul. But maybe I should use my time to have fun. That would make a nice change.

If I drift a little, it's fine. I am 'permitted', at times, to have some freedom - to move (a little), to think (a little) ... to daydream and fantasize. To imagine a world with no boundaries. No boat. Just me.

I would have no limits, restrictions, or constraints. There is no day or night, at least, not as we know it. Time can be as short or as long as I might decide it to be. I can go backwards, or forwards... or remain where I am. Whatever I decide, Me. My choices. There would be no responsibilities, except those that I pick. Not the ones that are given, or thrust upon me. I could choose to neglect the commitments I didn't ask to commit to or refuse the decisions that were made for me. I could renege on the family contracts I didn't sign up for, but, am obliged, and/or pressured to abide by.

Free from guilt.

Free from stress.

Free to be me again.

26

But I am the care giver. The Matriarch. The eldest. I am the parent; the mother and the father, the good, and the bad.

I often feel that I am swimming in different directions, caught in a current that can quickly turn into a riptide. I am constantly treading water and getting nowhere fast. I look around and I see so much, and yet, I have been nowhere. So, I look upwards at a cloudless sky, and I dream that I can fill all that space with whatever I want and with whoever I want. At the start it is difficult for me to picture these things, for I have been shackled to one thing or another for so long. Forced to keep my head down, keep focussed, be serious, be organised, be strong. But I am strong, yet I am also broken. Maybe someone will notice? I am running low on energy, so for now, I drift quietly and calmly. Drift as far as my chain and anchor will allow. Until the tug comes... gently, or as an almighty yank... forcing me back to reality.

I am just a little boat and somewhere through time I have become lost in this ocean. Perhaps then it is a good thing. Good that I am held in place; otherwise, I may simply float away and vanish. Imagine.

Perhaps the only way to my freedom is when my little boat can no longer stay afloat and sinks. Death.

Sometimes I hope, and I wait ... and I will welcome it.

Fighting Spirits
Jenny Pugsley, 78

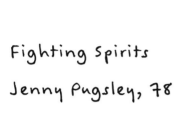

Mother was a Star. Born into what you might have called a genteel working-class family in London, in 1923, she was intelligent, lively – frivolous even, petite, with a beautiful face, but feared she was less loved than her more compliant elder sister. In this she was half-right only. All her life she was popular with men because she had a good sense of humour, while retaining a proper standard of behaviour for a woman of her time, and eventually a married woman (from 1942) and mother (1946). As she'd always been articulate in telling stories of the old days, I persuaded her to write them down, in round and rolling longhand, over some 50 pages of foolscap, which I typed up, then added photographs and had printed into a booklet in 2013.

I quote:

From Chapter 6: Harrods, 1938 – 1941: "I remember the Company laying on a portable gas chamber for us so that we could experience wearing our gas masks. So terrified were we, we all held our breath as we walked through, so we didn't know if the masks worked or not!"

From Chapter 7: The war years, 1939 – 1945/6: "I would be travelling into and out of central London every day for my job with the Ministry of War Transport {charting the movement of merchant ships}. It happened that I would come home and a whole street would have been demolished and our neighbours and friends killed. At night I would sometimes be needed to go out fire-watching in Barons Court {West London}, armed with only a tin helmet and a torch, looking for incendiary bombs. What would I do if I found one? Report it to the fire warden? Not the typical life of a teenager now."

From Chapter 9: Ministry of War Transport, 1941 – 1946: "It was some time after the end of the war that I learnt the dramatic events of Christmas 1944. Jack's {my father's, her husband's} regiment was taking part in the bombardment of Caen (the extreme noise of their heavy artillery was the start of Jack's hearing problems, which got worse over the years). This was followed by the famous Battle of the Bulge in the Ardennes in Belgium, with our allies the Canadians and the Americans. In retrospect, I now realise how traumatized men were after their experiences, and we did not fully understand how to help and deal with their demons. We young wives were still recovering from our own traumas. Back in "civvy street" there was no counselling in those days.

Jack was very reticent about his five years in the army and just wanted to forget, I guess. He was a very gentle man and, indeed, a gentleman."

As Charlotte's daughter, I struggle to think what I've achieved in my life against comparable odds! Do my first 30 years, notable for excruciating shyness, amount to a struggle? Does the care for my superb husband, over roughly seven years, at the end of his life, when his illness, Parkinson's, limited his physical and cognitive abilities but never his good temper or wit, really equate to a battle? For him, yes, for me, a challenge that I mostly felt up to. He had already turned my life, and my shyness, around, some 30 years previously. I had decided in my teens that I did not want to be a mother myself, but wanted to study languages, to work outside the home, in educational settings, with illuminating company, a level of responsibility and for a salary that would enable me to be financially independent and return something material to my parents. I got an excellent grammar school and university education at no real monetary cost to my parents or myself. My partner, and eventually husband, worked as hard as anyone I knew and not without stress, but we could travel for work and holidays when it was still safe and reasonably cheap to do so.

My mother was tough, tougher than I've had to be, and not always an easy opponent. I have her to thank for many things, for teaching me to read before primary school, for a sense of humour, the recognition that I was indeed loved, a deep emotional stamina, and her blue, blue eyes. And not least, her wisdom in marrying Jack! Their marriage of 64 years was a romance, as was mine to Roger, albeit only half that timespan. Their bench in the local Terrace Gardens gives a flavour of what they were.

Roger – "You made other people blossom." Charlotte and

Jack – "Fighting spirits, in wartime and in peace." I sometimes wonder if, and when, my war will come. Perhaps old age, without them, is it.

Reflections of Jenny (Ann) Pugsley, b. 1946, but mostly Charlotte Elizabeth Pugsley, b. 1923 - d. 2019.

Becoming 40
Serena Burton

I allowed myself a moment of elation as I twirled in front of our bedroom mirror, dressed in my sapphire blue silk dress and relieved that it fitted so well. I told my reflection that it was going to be a wonderful night for my 40th birthday party but my throat was dry with nerves.

Had I remembered everything? Hoping so, I sat down on the little curved sofa at the end of the bed and looked at the list of what we had ordered from a local Chinese restaurant that offered outside catering, with its exotic mixture of Chinese and a few European foods.

It seemed a good selection and it was too late now to change everything, so I stood up, put my shoulders back, walked into a huge living room, found my husband waiting patiently and did a twirl for him that made him laugh. Then he kissed me on the forehead and smiling at each other we headed out of our 26th floor, high rise apartment and into the beautiful warm Hong Kong Island evening.

The weather looked as if it was going to be kind as we sailed out of the bay of Aberdeen Harbour on a converted Chinese Junk. We were surrounded by some thirty or so of our friends and many newly acquired acquaintances, the women in their best party clothes, watching each other, smiling and assessing, manicured hands holding their glasses of champagne. Their partners looking desperate to take off their formal ties and unbutton their shirts.

One of my favourite pieces of classical music, Pachelbel's 'Canon and Gigue in D major' was playing softly on the CD player and the sound drifted out across the water as the sun started to set and the huge sky wore what looked like a mass of red curls as we headed towards Lantau Island.

My husband and I glanced fleetingly at each other with that intimate sense of warmth, knowing what the other was thinking. Yes, it was going to be okay.

Nothing is by Chance
- Shine Your Light

Harry Cannon, 79

Age UK Richmond's Choice Award ⭐

It was the early 1950s and the weekly piano lesson in town was well underway. As a young lad, I was forbidden any such lessons, most especially dancing. Grandfather ruled the roost. My mother would defy this ruling and drive me at speed into town to learn piano with a piano teaching cousin, Olga. On one occasion in mid lesson Grandfather drove up outside in his Humber on an unannounced visit. Quick thinking Olga unceremoniously bundled me into the cupboard under the stairs where I remained until Grandfather had gone.

From the very start it was not going to be ordinary...

For the first months after my birth, I spent my days in a wicker basket on the reception counter of a Caltex filling station. Later our family moved to a smallholding in the country. They were wonderful barefoot years with cats and dogs, a donkey, chickens and an array of produce from the garden. I rode bicycles down to the beach with my cousins, sometimes with my little Fox Terrier in a carrier box on the back or sat on the pillars of the driveway gate to see who could first spot the Sunday mail ship from the UK making its way up the coast. On special days, like the Queen's birthday, a sizeable Union Jack would be unfurled from the top of the water tower.

School was initially all classes together in an old garage and Sunday school Bible classes held by Mrs Bardwell of the Salvation Army in a garage behind the concrete replica of 'The Flying Dutchman'. Later school was in a purpose-built building.

To make extra pocket money I was allowed to launch a Pawpaw Project, planting the seeds, nurturing them to seedling stage and then with the gardener's help, planting them out in a field to grow and harvest the fruit. There were a hundred or so seedlings most of which would normally be female fruit bearing plants... except in this case after growing to maturity the whole planting yielded nothing but non fruit bearing male plants! No one, except the Universe of course, ever understood how that had happened. Nothing is by chance.

Against the rules, there were tap and modern dancing lessons too and elocution lessons, Eisteddfod and dance shows and plays were entered into with enthusiasm. I made a passable whirling North Wind once, with some kind soul winding away on a wind machine in the wings.

Then at 10 years old it was off to boarding school in Grahamstown. It was a Methodist Church school and that meant church twice every Sunday with a tradition of hearty singing from the balconies in the evening service.

I did the absolute bare minimum in compulsory rugby and cricket that rules would allow. Then I'd go off to piano lessons and play in school concerts. At break time when others made off to the field to kick balls around, I made a beeline for the little music room at the side of the stage in the Main Hall. The hall was filled with tables for meals and the headmaster and teachers sat at the table on the stage. Immersed in Liszt one day, I did not hear the lunch bell. There was suddenly a knock on the door and the headmaster stuck his head round. "Excuse me" he said, "the rest of the school is waiting for lunch!" I had to scuttle the full length of the hall to my seat with the lot of them standing waiting to say grace and smirking mercilessly. What an awful embarrassment.

And so it was that in my senior year at one morning assembly I sat and listened to the awards being read out... School Colours (for rugby, cricket, swimming, etc.) and then the ultimate Honours Awards (no headdress required when honours were worn). Neither of these awards had ever been given for other than sporting achievements. Suddenly everyone was looking at me aghast. Had my name been read out? Yes, it had, as an Honours award for Music, the first in the school's very long history. There were, of course, in the years that followed many more who were awarded Honours for Music at the school, recipients more accomplished than me but I was the first, a ground breaker and could be proud of that.

The lesson is perhaps that even one's most awfully embarrassing moments may not be what they seem. Ultimately none of it matters. Always, always be true to yourself. Be joyful in who you are and keep shining... nothing is by chance.

The light you shine will likely light the way for others.

Keep shining your light.

You are the star.

A Day At The Spa
Alexandra Kingston, 72

It may surprise you to know that I would rather go to the dentist than the hairdresser. Just. At least in the dentist's chair you are not required to make banal conversation with the junior shampooist, while she tries to form words with her painfully enlarged lips, discuss where you are going for your holiday or listen to nonsense about product, choppiness and movement. For the uninitiated, or bald, 'product' refers to industrial quantities of sticky gunk which is applied to your locks, at enormous cost, ensuring that your very expensive hairdo will look within 24 hours as though you had dipped your head in a paste bucket. Possibly sooner.

In an unsuccessful but caring attempt to create a spa-type feeling my dentist has invested in a fluffy blanket in which to cocoon her patients whilst they submit to her ministrations. I think it would have been churlish to remark that at her prices it should have been cashmere rather than polyester.

The hygienist, bad cop to good cop, doesn't even pretend you are there to have a good time. Her "I have to be cruel to be kind" is up there with "There's a cheque in the post" and "I hardly know the girl" in the scale of Great Lies of All Time. In an attempt to gain the psychological upper hand, I tell her that as she works, I am mentally composing an article about her sadism for international release, aka on my Facebook page. Adding that if you have already said "We're nearly there" ten times you are in danger of losing credibility. She didn't even blush.

I also announced that following a recent Big Birthday I would no longer be investing the annual GNP of a minor African nation in the maintenance of my teeth. I doubt, I announce, that at this point I am likely to reap the benefit, and I will savour the time saved in the frantic flossing that precedes every appointment in a pathetic attempt to convince them that this has been a twice daily habit since early childhood.

Like the parents of a willful toddler, they have seen it all before and aren't going to take any notice of today's tantrum, for which, secretly, I thank them. Without them I would have been reduced to an entirely liquid diet years ago although I increasingly move towards that in some senses. We have a laugh. I take them jars of home-made marmalade with labels instructing them to run it onto their gums. It really is more fun than the hairdresser. And better value.

Streetcar

by John O'Brien, 75

He had used the wrong oil. It was not deliberate, just one of those silly mistakes that get made when a man is tired, not paying full attention to the task in hand. With any other vehicle the mistake would not have had serious consequences, but streetcars, streetcars are a strange breed. Temperamental and particular about the way they are handled, streetcars react badly to the wrong lubrication. The oil overheated in the main bearing. The slip and slide, so necessary in a good oil, just ebbed away, leaving raw bearings, shearing hot metal to metal, welding the previous moving parts into a seized-up mass of static. This streetcar was going nowhere!

Desiré was a strange name to give to a male child, a decision made stranger by the eventual athletic prowess that the child developed. In his late teens he emerged as one of Africa's finest young footballers. Though pronounced by family and friends and those in the know, to rhyme with cabaret or tourniquet or even Mandalay, Desiré suffered continual annoyance when fans, for and against, chanted his name to rhyme with retire, conspire or fire. In fact, some poetic away fans even struck up the chant of "It's time to retire desire". Poor prospects for a future career in management were predicted by his given name, but to magnify the unusual nature of his first name, the young man inherited the family name of Job. Not Job as in "give us a job", but Job, as in "take off my robe" – Job, the Old Testament wiseman renowned for his patience.

Job was late and the traffic was slow and heavy. A man built for speed is annoyed more than most by a snail's pace progression towards the objective. He reached the turn and waited impatiently for the streetcar to pass the junction so that he could make his turn onto the highway and regain some of the lost time.

It stopped. Right in front of him, the streetcar ground to a halt, smoke billowing from the rear wheel. He was completely blocked. The cars behind him, also waiting eagerly for their chance to hit the highway, were bumper to bumper. He could not move.

He got out of his car as the passengers rushed and jostled their way off the smoking streetcar. The driver, barking instructions to keep calm, was ignored by all. Desiré guessed that the problem was with the rear wheel. He had a fire extinguisher in the car and running forward, pulled the pin, cracked the handle and sent a white cloud of expellant that engulfed the rear wheel. The flames subsided, the smoke stopped, and the crowd gathered round to find out what was happening. Desiré rolled on his back and edged in under the streetcar to examine the problem. He could not wait all day for a breakdown truck to remove the obstruction.

As he reached up towards the seized bearing, the streetcar lurched forward crushing his leg. Screams from the crowd were not loud enough to cover the howls of pain from the injured footballer.

She poured her coffee as if on auto pilot, following the pre-ordained path of early morning ritual developed over the years. The first morning cigarette was the one thing she had worked hard to erase from her morning routine. The unexpected discovery of high blood pressure some three years back demanded changes. Coffee, no cream, and dry toast were now the start of the day for her.

Dry toast, dry toast - surely that would give you high blood pressure from the sheer annoyance of no butter.

She moved to the table on her balcony, collecting the morning newspaper as she went. The headline caught her eye. It was unusual. It had a slight déjà vu about it. She mouthed the words slowly to herself. "Streetcar maimed Desiré".

"What's that all about?" she asked herself.

Chicken Surprise

Pamela-Marie Lumbroso, 67

This happened several years ago.

On the invitation of some friends, I flew from London to Hyderabad, India with my four children for a visit and to have an adventure. We were all excited and looking forward to it as we had never been there before. It was a long trip, but we arrived safely, and the children were model travellers.

Once we adjusted to the heat, and I got over my fear of the buffaloes that passed our house each evening, we really enjoyed being there. It was like a wonderland.

The spicy balmy smell of incense, rich and woody. Swirling upwards with the prayers of the faithful.

Masala chai, fruity milky tea laced with warming spices and ginger.

The hiss of sizzling oil fried treats, filling your nostrils with a warm, yet slightly oily sensation. And the promise of sweetness.

Market stalls laden with spices that fill the air with zingy cumin, dusty cinnamon, the oomph of mustard seeds, powerful peppercorns, robust bay leaves, and the fiery vigour of chillies, (there is one spice that took some getting used to, acrid Asafoetida!).

The pungent smell of curry that lingers around you and on you.

The fragrance of fresh sun ripened mangoes, juicy, fleshy and delicious.

Sugar cane being pressed over ice, its bark opening to reveal the sticky sweet goodness within.

Jasmine flowers with their heady floral scent, woven into garlands or adornments for the hair. The Buttery sweet aroma of coconut oil, embellishing the hair and making it shine.

Smoky burning mosquitos' coils, herbal and citrusy. A tolerable scent to us, but deadly to them.

The loud, bright, scintillating fireworks of Diwali.

This story is something funny that happened due to my misunderstanding.

Mark and Martine were going to hold a thank you dinner for some of the donors who contributed to their charity, and I was tasked with ringing round for a butcher to provide some chickens.

Amazingly, I found one quite quickly who was eager to not only help with the amount requested but he offered them free of charge! We agreed on a time for them to be delivered. "I got them!", I said triumphantly as I hung up the phone.

The day came and I went to answer the doorbell. I greeted the poulterer at the door and confirmed this was the correct address. He returned to his vehicle to retrieve the chickens while I went to the kitchen to get some bags.

We met at the door. I looked at him in utter amazement, he looked back at me with a grin as my bags dropped slowly to the floor.

Well! There he stood holding several chickens all tied together by their feet.

"Where do you want them?" he asked me. "They are very fresh."

I was speechless. I pointed to a space under the marble staircase.

Mark and Martine came downstairs, and I must have looked clearly shocked.

"I thought they'd be oven ready and covered in cling film!" I stuttered. I felt like a fool. And we all had a good laugh.

But all was not lost. A local butcher agreed to pick them up right away and prepare them in exchange for keeping the feathers.

And yes, the dinner was a success and the chickens were delicious!

The Rainbow
Susan Weaver

Remembering Wg.Cdr. Cyril Pover, OBE, DFC

My father, born in 1922, joined the Royal Air Force in 1941 and by January 1942 he was a Sergeant Pilot flying Wellington Bombers. In 1944 he attended a promotion interview with the notoriously shy Leonard Cheshire VC. Without once looking up from his desk, he said "So, Povey, why do you want to become an officer?" Whatever he replied must have worked because he left with the rank of pilot officer. A successful career with the RAF followed, flying and instructing on many types of aircraft and occupying senior positions in Rhodesia, Aden and Singapore, retiring in 1968.

A significant posting was to RAF Leconfield, Yorkshire, the base of 640 Halifax Squadron where at the tender age of 22 he was captaining several flights over Germany. One, particular relevant to this story, was in the night/morning of 28/29 November 1944

"Target Essen" - bombing the Krupp Steelworks.

One day, early 90s, he was contacted by his wireless operator who persuaded him to attend a reunion at Leconfield. He was not one for reunions as so many of the bomber crews failed to return and the memory was often too much to attend these reunions.

They stayed locally at the brewery at the Beverley Arms which brought back memories of snatched beers on the rare occasion they were off the airfield. There followed an emotional day visiting all the places which had hardly changed in the 50 years since Leconfield was a busy operational station. He described the church where he would watch girls packing parachutes and hoping that his would never be needed.

Then there was Nissen Hut, where crews gathered for their operational briefings, the red telephone box and finally the runway.

At the reunion he was given a cassette of an original and unique BBC wire recording of the operational briefing for that night raid on Essen. He was particularly proud as his name was mentioned as the leader of one of the waves of bombers leaving the base at night. Many failed to return next morning. He brought the cassette home, gathered the family around and we listened.

After his death in 1996, my friend transferred the cassette to CD cleaning up crackles and labelling it - a great gift. As I had expressed a wish to follow Cyril's footsteps around the base, in early "22 he arranged for us to be shown around Leconfield (by then an Army transport and RAF rescue base).

We were first taken to the church (run by the Army Padre). Alongside was the parachute packing station with its tower for drying the chutes and where Cyril had watched those girls with eagle eyes in case of any mistakes.

Next the red telephone box on a grassy mound near the church. Attached to the door were the remains of a padlock hasp, painted over and almost invisible. Our guide invited us to guess what it was for. His answer was shocking. Just before a raid was announced, the door was locked. They simply could not risk the boys calling home to say when and where they were going. The thought of them going out and possibly not returning without having been able to tell anyone was so sad.

Then came the Nissen Hut. It was still there because it was a listed building and now used as a campus cinema. This was the actual hut where the pre-raid briefings were conducted for the bomber crews.

It was empty with the exception of a projectionist high up at the back. Unbeknownst to me, my friend had hit on the idea of playing the briefing CD. I was sitting in the middle of that church, mind totally focused on being Cyril amongst those boys, probably nervous, cold but wrapped in their leather jackets and smoking, when suddenly it all came alive. The ghostly 1944 voice of the CO, the target, the route, the weather, the Flak, the night fighters, and all the time the nervous coughing and shuffling of seats. "Pilot Officer Povey would be leading the 5th wave at 5:00 AM next morning. Destination Essen." Hearing the actual voices in the actual place was more emotional than I can describe. The tears flowed. I had to be prized from my seat for the final surprise - runway.

We drove out to the threshold from where Cyril and his friends had taken off numerous times. I stood at the start of the vast wide concrete one runway in the rain, alone with my thoughts, imagining waves of the huge Halifax bombers thundering off into the night. When suddenly the rain cleared, and an incredible rainbow appeared on the far end of the runway. Tears flowed again. I believe he was telling me something. It surely was a sign that he was with me.

The Story of Mambo
Sarah Nekesa

Angela Rippon's Choice Award

One morning, my late father arrived home from the market with four goats. The rains from the previous night had softened the volcanic, fertile soils that made the slopes and valleys of Mt. Elgon perfect for growing Arabica coffee. Among the goats was a young and striking animal with a brown coat and a sporty black pattern around its neck.

The moment my late mother saw this peculiar goat, it seemed to recognize her immediately and followed her into the banana plantation. My mother turned to the goat and said, "Mambo", as if greeting a friend, and from that moment on, the young goat was named Mambo.

My mother fed Mambo banana peels and leftover vegetable husks. Mambo quickly became her favourite and followed her everywhere. Unlike the other animals—cows, sheep, and goats— that were sent down the valley to graze, Mambo preferred to stay close to my mother, finding comfort in her presence.

Whether my mother was working in the coffee and banana plantations, weeding grass, or planting crops, Mambo would be right by her side. Even when my mother sat down to peel bananas or light a fire, Mambo would sit next to her. The villagers were intrigued by the bond between my mother and this unusual goat.

As Mambo grew, she began to eat leaves, green beans, and grass around the compound, thriving under my mother's care. In a matter of months, she became pregnant and gave birth to triplets. Remarkably, each of Mambo's pregnancies resulted in twins or triplets, leading to a rapid increase in the number of goats in our household. My family sold some of the offspring and gave others to relatives, but Mambo remained a constant presence in our lives.

Mambo's bond with my mother was extraordinary. She even followed her to church and attended traditional ceremonies, becoming a familiar sight in the community. Over time, Mambo began to show signs of aging, and my parents debated what to do with her.

My father suggested slaughtering her, but my mother couldn't bear the thought. She preferred that Mambo be given away or sold rather than killed. Eventually, my father decided to sell Mambo to a relative, which meant she would leave our home. However, a week later, to everyone's surprise, Mambo found her way back to us.

Despite her return, the relative who had purchased Mambo came to take her back, as he had already paid for her. My mother was heartbroken to see Mambo go, feeling as though she was losing a dear friend.

Those who knew Mambo didn't want her to be sold, and her departure left a void in our lives. My family was sad but also reluctant to learn what ultimately happened to Mambo, the mysterious goat who had been such a close companion to my mother.

The memory of Mambo has never faded from my mind. Her story is one of loyalty and friendship, and it left us with many unanswered questions about the mysterious bond between a woman and her goat.

Even now, I often think of Mambo, and the extraordinary connection she shared with my mother remains one of the most cherished memories of my life.

The Storm

Elizabeth Cotrulia, 92

Tom was 10 years old when his mom took him on a holiday to the coast of Ireland. To a fishing town called Killyleagh.

The cottage they took for the holiday was in a lonely place of mountains and sea. At night it was cozy when the turf fire was lit. The weather was good, and the days were warm and sunny. It was just the right place for walking and climbing and exploring. Tom also liked to paint, and he was very good at it. Tom's mother was hoping this holiday would help him now that they were on their own. She wanted to give him as much freedom as possible. Tom missed his dad and wondered what was going to happen now that his parents were going to separate. He felt sad about the whole thing and didn't want to think about it, it was too painful.

Tom went to bed at 10 most nights and he didn't mind. He was tired from all the activities of the day. As he lay in bed, he wondered who the young pretty girl was in the faded photograph. He felt the girl with the sad eyes was looking down at him. He knew she was someone who had long departed from this world. Her spirit seemed so strong it almost frightened him. He fell asleep at last but was woken by the sound of the furious storm. The wind roared down the chimney and there was a frantic noise from the sea. When all the noises had died down, he could hear crying. There was a kind of hush sound, as if the night was holding its breath. There were footsteps at the back door. He could hear the beating of his heart. He ran downstairs to his mum.

"Quick, mum", he said. "Come up to my bedroom. There's something going on. I think there's somebody up there."

"Don't be silly Tom, I'm sure you're having a nightmare", his mum said. "I heard someone crying", said Tom. "Come and sit down by the fire, while I get you some hot milk. Then back to bed." "But what about the noises and the crying?"

"It's only the wind", his mum said again. He could still hear the waves beating against the cliffs and the storm was raging high. His mum tucked him in. "No more dreams, Tom. Sleep well."

Strangely enough, he did go back to sleep, and he didn't have any more dreams. The next day they set out to Sean Hennessy's shop, the man who they rented the cottage from. The day was calm and bright, and they could see the different colours of the sea. Pink, blue and light green as they walked along the beach.

"Having a good time?" Sean Hennessy asked as he loaded up their shopping bag. "It's not too melancholic for you up there, now that the height of the season is over?" "Oh, no! We love it, and it's such a lovely cottage," said Tom's mum. "You've some beautiful furniture there, Mr. Hennessy."

"Call me Sean. It's all the family stuff, you know", he said.

54

"The Hennessey families have lived in the colleges for years. They were all fishing folk; I was the same until I gave it up for this lot, now I'm not sure I did the right thing."

"Who is the young girl in the faded photo?" Tom asked.

"She was my grand uncle's wife", said Sean. "She was very pretty and very young when she married my great uncle. It's a very lovely, lonely place to live on your own and my grand uncle could be away for months at sea", said Sean.

"The story goes that she became friendly with one of the young lads from the nearby farm and later they became lovers. When my grand uncle found out about it, he was so mad he said he would kill the lad."

"She ran out of the cottage that night and was never seen again. Some people say she was washed away by the storm. The funny thing was her body was never found."

That's some story Sean, said Tom's mum.

My father said she always returned when there was a storm. He would have it that she wanted to get in touch with her lover.

Years later, Tom won a prize for his painting of the girl with sad eyes, which had stayed in his memory all this time. He related to the girl and the sad story as the two people who he had loved the most were parting, which he found very hard to take. He now realized people don't always stay together for life, sometimes they part for the best reasons and at the time Tom found it so difficult to accept. What is important now is that he knows his parents loved him, and that will never change.

Retirement Day
- A New Chapter

Tim Rolls, 67

Births, marriages, deaths, illnesses, family events, house moves and other key events populate lives, but certain other landmark days stand out as important chapters in many people's life stories.

First day at school. Nerves. New uniform. Huge new building. New classmates. Scary teachers. School dinners. Everything seems big and frightening.

Last day at school. Adult life stretching ahead. Opportunities. Possibilities. Ambitions. Excitement.

First day at work. More nerves. The need to get to know both your job and your colleagues. Earning money. Independence. Being a grown-up.

Last day at work. For many a time of worry. Reduced financial circumstances and social contact. Concerns about how to fill the spare time. Or, maybe, a chance to start a new, flourishing life chapter.

After 22 years with the same company, in a job I was increasingly at odds with, I was made redundant in my mid-fifties. Redundancy money, a company pension plus my wife still working meant that with some trimming we could survive financially without me needing to work again, obviously a fortunate position to be in. I therefore faced the challenge of what to do with the rest of my life, and, crucially, how to keep my brain active. I could let events take their course or try to steer my own path. Happily, I chose the latter option, and I look back on the day I retired as one of the most momentous of my life.

It's over a decade since my retirement. Without stressing myself too much, and with plenty of space in my diary for family and other important activities, I've managed to keep myself pretty much fully occupied. I did an Open University social science degree. I helped set up, and chaired for four years, a Chelsea FC supporters organisation. I could have managed neither of these if I was still working.

I'd always wanted to write and, crucially, within a year of retirement I started writing articles for a Chelsea supporters' magazine. This led to conversations with a publisher, which in turn led to me having three books on Chelsea history published, with two more in the pipeline. I had barely written anything apart from work stuff since I left school in 1975, so this was a completely new avenue for my energies. Taking writing further, I recently did an 'Introduction to Creative Writing Course' with a view to producing short stories and have just signed up for a more advanced course. In some ways I treat writing as a job, and indeed I now describe myself as 'a writer' (as opposed to 'retired') but, importantly, I start or stop as I wish. I have deadlines but they are largely self-imposed. If I wish to spend the afternoon reading in the garden or going for a walk with my wife, I do. She is also retired and a full-time artist, utilising creative skills she's always possessed but lacked the time to exploit.

The other crucial thing I did was take up walking football five years ago, through Age UK Richmond. Excellent for my physical health, important in that it gives twice-weekly social contact with a large group of others of a similar age, it quickly became a key part of my week. I was never talented and if you'd said to me thirty years ago that I'd still be playing regularly in my late sixties, I would have laughed. But here we are.

Activities need not cost a lot of money. Writing costs nothing, walking football £5 a session. Volunteering costs nothing. Age UK and other organisations run a wide array of different activities where you can interact with others whilst receiving physical and/or mental benefits.

If you are about to retire, embrace it, treat it as an opportunity, try to make it work for you. Life will sometimes get in the way of plans – I had to deal with the passing of both my parents, for example – but activities can give a structure to your week, keep your brain fertile, get you out and about and, without causing stress, get you out of your comfort zone. Yes, there are con-straints – health, money, mobility, responsibilities – but there are often ways of working round them.

I'll be honest. I feared I might slowly fossilise in retirement, time rich but activity poor. The reality is I'm as busy as I want to be, have more of a sense of achievement than I did for much of my working life and, most of the time, enjoy myself. If that's the case with me, it could be with you. Identify things you want to do, or try to do, and have a go.

The day you retire should not be the end, but a new beginning.

My Wedding Day
Roberta Jack, 78

3rd July, 1966. My Wedding Day. I woke up, saw my wedding dress hanging outside my wardrobe and felt a wave of nausea go through me. For 2 reasons: 1) I knew I was marrying the wrong man. I didn't love him, he didn't love me. I was marrying him because my mother told me to. What his motives were, l had no idea. And 2) Everyone would be looking at me FOR THE WHOLE DAY!

While I was getting dressed my aunt came in and decided that was the best time to tell me what to expect on my wedding night. Only she didn't explain fully. She told me, in great detail, the facts of rape. So it was with great trepidation that I went downstairs to meet my guests.

The first indication that things would not be going smoothly was when the florist came with the flowers... and the explanation that instead of orchids for the mothers she had sent some

60

extra carnations. OK, no problem, both mothers agreed that they would wear two carnations each instead of orchids.

Until the mothers went upstairs to dress and came back to find that, although they lived 3,000 miles apart, had never met before and each had chosen and made their costumes themselves, they both wore identical outfits in exactly the same colour. Okay...

Then the cars arrived to take the guests to the synagogue. My father had ordered a Rolls-Royce to take himself and me, and five other cars for the guests. But... the garage owner called to say he was very sorry, but all his "normal" cars had been booked for that day, so he was sending us...five Bentleys instead! The sight of a Rolls-Royce and five Bentleys standing outside our house (and probably half-way up the street) must have caused many curtains to twitch.

Eventually all the guests had been taken, together with both mothers and the groom's father, and the Rolls Royce went to collect the groom, take him to the synagogue and return for my father and myself. Dad and I waited... and waited... and waited. But the Rolls didn't come back. At one time the neighbours were treated to the sight of my father and myself, in all my wedding finery, pacing the front garden looking for the missing car. Finally, dad phoned the garage to try and get some information, to be told that the Rolls-Royce had returned to the garage, having been told that there was no-one else to come! Dad quickly put that right and within ten minutes the Rolls was at the door. As he drove us to the synagogue the driver explained what had happened. Apparently, he had picked up the groom and asked him if there was anyone else to collect. The groom, thinking that he

61

meant from his house, said no, there was nobody else to come, so the driver returned to the garage, along with the five Bentleys.

My father then realised that the driver was taking the "scenic" route to the synagogue, all through the town and along the seafront. On being asked why, the driver told him that this was usual for a wedding car, so that people could see the bride. As we were already over an hour late, dad told him to just hurry up and go directly to the synagogue.

On arrival at the synagogue, dad and I were taken to a side room to wait while the groom, whom the rabbi had locked in his office while he investigated why the bride had apparently 'gone missing', was released and brought to stand under the bridal canopy. My father and I were then told it was time. And my father started a slow march, a funeral march, down the aisle. I tried to hurry him along, but dad wouldn't be hurried. It had to be slow and stately. We eventually arrived at the bottom of the two steps leading up to the bridal canopy and I put my right foot forward to take the first step. Only to find that I had trodden on the hem of my wedding dress, forcing me to bend my knee; unable to free my foot from my dress, and my father dragging me up the second step, I arrived under the canopy almost on my knees. Dad finally let go of my arm and I straightened up and glanced at my groom, to see him red of face and sweating profusely. This was worrying; I could understand him being nervous, but sweating? And red? I could only think of one reason: he was going to say No. OK by me, but embarrassing, nonetheless. He didn't.

Encounter With a
Prehistoric Beast -
Uganda 1961

Richard Wellesley, 90

Dr Russell Schechter's Choice Award ⭐

The road from Kampala to Jinja winds its way eastwards through very beautiful scenery, with dense jungle on the left and occasional glimpses of Lake Victoria on the right. After a journey of about 30 miles the road arrives at a long bridge which crosses over the Ripon Falls — the exact point where Lake Victoria empties itself dramatically and noisily into the White Nile, giving off a fine mist visible from miles around. Immediately after crossing the bridge, a fork in the road to the right takes one along a narrow suburban road, with European style houses on the left with extensive gardens, and a golf course on the right — the golf course bordering the lake itself.

I was on a two-month stint in Kampala and had been invited

to a party in Jinja. At about 7.00 o'clock in the evening as night was beginning to fall, I saw a huge hippopotamus emerging on the left from one of the gardens. I stopped the car and waited for a few minutes, hoping for the beast to move away. But the animal was hungry and enjoying munching the flowers at the edge of the road. After ten minutes or so, feeling ready for my first whisky, I decided to get past him. Big mistake! As I was alongside him he took off at incredible speed. Lumbering along beside me at about 30 mph he towered over my small and flimsy 'Beetle' Volkswagen. Weighing about one and a half tons he would have been nearly twice as heavy as my VW Beetle which with a small air-cooled engine was one of the lightest cars on the road at that time. Had he decided to barge into me he would definitely have been able to flip the car. As it was, I decided, in spite of my competitive instincts which were ordering me to race him, and bearing in mind that news of injuries or death incurred competing with a hippo would take a lot of swallowing in Gillette HQ, that discretion should be the better part of valour. I slowed, and, seizing his opportunity, the hippo swung in front of me and careered across the golf course towards the lake.

Recounting my story at the party, slightly light-headed, whisky at last in hand, expecting a rapt audience, I was informed by the expats that encounters with hippopotami in Jinja were a regular occurrence; hippos considered gardens to be their luxury restaurants and lakeside residents accepted this as a fact of life. However, the same expats did give me some advice, which I have since always observed (well once, in South Africa) and will pass on, for their edification and future application, to any readers of this memoir. 'Never EVER try to do anything to try to cut off a hippo's route back to his home the water'. My hippo had assumed I was trying to do exactly that, and that's what made him go so ballistic.

Granny, I Hardly Knew You

Rosie Jackson, 76

Photo in 1949 or 1950. No color, black, white and grey. An elderly woman, Granny Jackson, holding a toddler in her arms. Me. A year or so old, staring blandly, uncertainly, at Granny for the first, last time. This being my only visit to Northern Ireland.

In England, a year or so on, a knock at our front door, Dad had invited his father, Grandpa Jackson, over to visit us. Granny Jackson has died. I'm not quite sure what died means, except you go away for a long time and aren't ever seen again. Also, people are sad.

A man is at the front door. Grandpa. A woman stands nervously to one side and slightly behind him. Dad seemed shocked and on the edge. Who is this woman? Who is she? Something isn't right. I don't know what it is. Fierce mutterings between Dad and Grandpa. Much unease. Eventually Dad lets them in. I'm told emphatically only to call the woman Aunt Lizzie.

66

It's a two-bedroom house. Suddenly all three of us, mum, dad and I are squashed into the front bedroom. I fall asleep, finally, to the rhythm of my parents. OK. But urgent exchanges on the day's happenings? Meanwhile, Grandpa Annalize retired quietly to the back bedroom.

Next day they disappear to visit London. They returned home that evening and presented me with a silver charm bracelet. I'm delighted. My mum tells me that the clock charm is Big Ben, the very important clock that makes sure everyone knows the right time. Another charm shows some ballet shoes. Ballerinas dance on the stage in London. I shake the charms on the bracelet. My father says nothing.

Early next morning I woke to an explosion of noise downstairs. I run out onto the landing and stare down through the banisters. Why am I not in the middle of this excitement? Why are they ignoring me? I creep down the stairs quietly not to be left out. They haven't seen me, but I slipped on the last few stairs and found myself on the floor. In the middle of the melee.

As I raised my arm, my father spotted the little silver charm bracelet still on my wrist. And you can take this back. He shouts as he wrenched it from my wrist. It isn't Lizzie. I protest and struggle but it's an uneven contest. I recall it like a snake, but I am crying now.

'At least let the child keep the bracelet.' Please Aunt Lizzie. Why don't they like her? She seems a nice lady, but they can't say my father has ordered it. So, they pack their bags and go taking the bracelet with them.

As they leave, my father says begrudgingly to Grandpa in a

part of act of contrition, "If you come on your own some other time, you can stay, but not with that woman and my mother not yet cold in her grave".

Grandpa never came again. I lost him as well as the rest of any extended family in Northern Ireland on that day, along with the silver charm bracelet.

The Exchange
Janet Hughes

They say you always remember your first love. Mine was France. From the moment I stepped off the boat and was met by my exchange student I felt at home. France felt like home as England never did.

When we walked through the streets of her small hometown in Normandy, the aroma of French cooking on the air was unforgettable. To a teenager brought up on post-war rationing and unimaginative English food it was a revelation. Long, leisurely meals with home-made dishes (how I can still remember the beignets that Madame made!) and wine with everything. It was the start of living to eat, French-style.

Being a teenager, it was also the start of romance. Of course, what else? France and Frenchmen are famous for it. During that first visit we went camping, which I have always hated, but it was a far cry from the Guide camps of my childhood. French sophistication filtered here, with the boys fixing up electric lights around our tents. They were men already, smoking Gitanes and Gauloises and squinting meaningfully through the smoke with a film-star air. And, yes, I fell for one of them and he for me.

It was interesting, many years later, to discover that some of my ancestors were Vernons, people who originally came to England with William the Conqueror, and when first in France I had visited the nearby Normandy town of Vernon. Was this a coincidence or destiny? Could my feeling of coming home to France be an ancestral memory from those who went before me? A cell memory, my Welsh cousin, steeped in Celtic mysticism, would say.

Strangely enough, it was my cousin who ended up spending most of her life in Paris, whilst I lived and worked in Geneva, which, though French-speaking, lacked the atmosphere of my beloved France.

In the following years, though I spent holidays in France, I never managed to make a life there and never really felt that England is home.

And the young Frenchman? Well, we spent a few years corresponding and criss-crossing the Channel, but life – National Service, university – got in the way. And, this time contrary to what they say, absence did not make the heart grow fonder.

Walking in Mallorca

Karin McLean

After a hearty breakfast in the hotel, we were booted and suited to go on our walk from Port de Soller situated at the foot of the Serra de Tramuntana mountains to Deia. It is known for its literary and musical residents. The poet Robert Graves lived and was buried there. We first stopped at Maria's grocery shop to buy our lunch; a bocadillo (a little baguette cut in half sprayed with olive oil, topped with ham, local cheese and tomato), apples and water.

We set off uphill on the mule track to the lighthouse where you had a stunning view of the horseshoe bay of the port. We then followed the path, red dots on rocks and trees and cairns guiding us in the right direction. We passed olive groves, mules showed no interest in us, fortunately. Mid-morning we arrived at an old finca where we had freshly squeezed orange juice and a piece of cake freshly baked in the morning by the grandmother.

Once our batteries recharged, we continued our walk. We

stopped from time to time to take in the stunning views, take pictures and have lunch. We walked up and down the path, stepped over stiles watching carefully where we put our feet. The path is not smooth, sometimes even close to the edge of the cliffs. It is very quiet, we only heard the twittering of birds and the bells on the necks of the free roaming goats and sheep.

Early afternoon we arrived at Cala de Deia, a small beach. It took our tiring legs about twenty minutes to wander uphill to the village. It is not large but it has a taverna where we enjoyed a cold beer. At about 4 o'clock we went to the bus stop to take the bus back to Port de Soller. To our surprise there were plenty of other tourists waiting. Where did they come from? We hardly saw anybody on our walk.

The bus arrived more or less on time. When we wanted to step on the bus the driver said "sorry no more, the bus is full". We asked when the next bus is due. The driver answered "in four hours. There is a taxi rank over there, you can always take a taxi". We found the taxi rank but no taxi. There was, however, a notice with the telephone number. We called the number and spoke to the taxi driver. "Can you pick us up please from Deia to take us to Port de Soller?" The driver answered "I'd love to but I am on holiday in Barcelona".

There we were, what to do, walking back was not an option, we were too tired. It was a long wait for the next bus and the risk of it being full again was a great possibility. We remembered there was a luxury hotel, La Residencia, previously owned by Richard Branson. We tried our luck and went to the reception of the hotel. A blackboard announcing they were serving afternoon tea did not much get our attention and did not tempt us. We wanted to get back to the hotel. The receptionist ordered a taxi which arrived in ten minutes. She did not even ask whether we were guests in the hotel. We arrived back at our hotel relieved, in time for a refreshing shower, a rest and a delicious dinner laughing with our little adventure of the day.

Nora's Gift

Howard Friend, 75

My grandmother was psychic, according to my mother. "The Irish are closer to the spirit world", she would say. Nora, my grandmother, was from Clonmel-on-Suir, Co Tipperary. As a girl, she worked in what she called the Big House there (probably Knocklofty, seat of the Earl of Donoughmore), as ancient snapshots demonstrate, always well-dressed because she was regularly handed on the chatelaine's nearly new cast-offs. In service, she lived with her rich family, if the 1911 Irish Census is accurate, returning occasionally to her parents. Her father was a gardener among a large family in O'Neill Street. There was a brother Micky who enlisted and was killed in action, and various sisters, one of whom drank vinegar, another who would wash the baby's bottom under a standpipe outside the house. Nora was closest to another sister, Mary.

There, in Clonmel, Nora met an English soldier garrisoned

in the town in 1913. After his four years of service in France, they married. Contrary perhaps to expectation, my grandfather, Charles, was loved by Nora's Catholic family, a fully reciprocated affection. He found work in Ireland but with too little reward for a young family and, after similar luck back in England, they eventually emigrated to Australia with my mother, Phyllis, and three siblings in tow. After WW2, Phyllis returned to Blighty on her own, met my father, an RAAF officer, on board ship, married in haste and repented at leisure. Father bought a characterless dwelling in Kenton, Middlesex, on the understanding that his Air Force London posting would eventually end and he would return to Sydney, this time with a family. Thus, we boarded SS Orion in 1953, arriving six weeks later in Sydney. Neither parent remained long Down Under, returning separately, my father departing without a word, then posting abject letters to Phyllis via his mother in Sydney, so that we would not know he had fled to England. Phyllis left with her two infants in 1955, later back to the temporary home in Kenton, Middlesex that had meanwhile been rented out to US servicemen with names like Dwight and Woody.

Some years later, the unhappy union seemed further blighted when Phyllis lost her engagement ring. On a day during our school holidays, she had gone off to work, inexplicably leaving the ring on a polished table with my sister and me at home all day, mere children, as well as two of our classmates, Ann and Janet Pounce, who called round in the afternoon. We four went off to the park, having made up jam sandwiches for a picnic. When we returned to the house, the ring had disappeared. My sister and I were innocent, as surely were our two quaint, churchgoing friends. Floorboards came up, the lot. Gone without a trace. This sentimental loss affected Phyllis deeply and immediately, to the point of taking a day off work. In a day or so, a rare telegram arrived from Nora in Sydney: "Is everything all right?" Phyllis thought this extraordinary evidence of Nora's psychic powers. We none of us stopped to ask why, by the same supernatural gift, Nora was not called upon to locate the missing item of jewellery, but perhaps that thought is just the cynicism of old age.

Then there was Betty Smith, in WW2 a fellow private in the WRAAC with Phyllis, nursing at the military hospital in Goulburn NSW. Surrounded by the battle-injured and dependent Allied naval officers and ratings, the nurses were in the right place for wartime romance. Betty, alas, was the one always left on the shelf, as they used to say.

Things worked out well for Betty, though, and in the mid-50s, by then married happily, she visited Phyllis, temporarily back in Australia. I remember the still youthful Betty chatting with Phyllis: ten or so years on, old colleagues and mainly pen pals. There was a little boy. They went home after tea, living in a different part of Sydney and then rather faded from Phyllis' life.

On a morning a year or so later, Nora said to my mother "I had an upsetting dream last night: your friend Betty Smith was with my sister Mary". Mary had died long ago, back in Clonmel. Just a dream, Phyllis thought. By post next day came a letter to Phyllis from Betty's husband. He was sorry to tell her that Betty was dying and, in the way of the times, urged my mother not to think about visiting as Betty's illness was at an advanced stage.

Phyllis, of course, wrote back in the following days, asking after her old army colleague. Betty's husband replied that, by the time Phyllis would have received his earlier letter, Betty had already died. Indeed, she died during the night of Nora's disturbing dream.

A Magic Moment
Sarah Wills

Age UK Richmond's Choice Award ⭐

It was a long time ago. I was young. I was in love. It was Paris. There were six of us together, there in that carefully chosen, expensive restaurant. I was the only woman, and I was not complaining. On the menu great food, a decent wine, good company, laughter, conviviality and as the main course... REVENGE! If we played our cards right, it would be a fitting payback for past transgressions of our intended victim. This otherwise decent, affable and empathetic colleague had established a deserved reputation for meanness. He was as tight as two coats of paint.

Despite a "No questions asked" expenses account, wherever a bill was presented much fumbling would ensue in his futile attempts to locate the entrance to his wallet. Seemingly baffled by some unremembered code, he would continue his farcical efforts until exasperation prompted the others to dismiss his efforts and the bill would be settled without his contribution. At this, the wallet was swiftly returned to its hiding place with a murmured apologetic "my turn next time." Predictably, that "next time" never came.

This special meal was drawing to a close. As a fitting end, liquors were ordered, toasts exchanged, and bonhomie prevailed.

With a tentative leap into the unknown, I chose the now forbidden Absinthe, that green, fiery, acrid drink so beloved of the artist colonies of yesteryear. A lighter was produced, and emerald flames spurted from the glass. This was no drink for sissies. A heady brew, potent enough to be an instant corpse reviver. One sip and I understood why.

And now the time had come. Our carefully laid plans were in place and the denouement approached. One by one, on various pretexts, we sidled from our table - to make a phone call (back then mobile phones were unknown), to congratulate the Maitre D', to request a copy of the menu for some non-existent recipient, etc.

To the pre-selected upper floor we scampered, and there, from the perfectly positioned window, we could gleefully observe proceedings with impunity.

Our victim, now seated alone, looked around vaguely, perplexed, confused. He stared at the wall, at the pictures hanging there, as though expecting at least one of us to emerge from within these framed portraits of some long-gone notables of yesteryear.

Slowly, realisation dawned. We were not coming back!

Again and again, he checked the bill while waiters discreetly hovered. Amazement followed by incredibility followed by something approaching horror as his eyes fastened upon the enormous bill which was now his and his alone.

Eventually his trembling fingers found their way to that seldom opened wallet, a wad of notes extracted. He watched in sorrow as they cascaded down to the table along with a cheque to supplement insufficient funds. Signed with a shaking hand.

With a rueful smile and a shrug of his shoulders, he gestured to the waiting staff that they should accept his payment, with a generous tip. A tale of the unexpected was unfolding before our eyes.

It was as though he had recognised the conspirators as a bunch of pranksters, he had been well and truly set up. Game, set and match acknowledged. He chuckled, raised his hand as though in salute and disappeared into the night.

And now it was time for us to leave. A few final reminiscences of the evening's events. Goodbyes were said, handshakes exchanged whereupon we dispersed and went our separate ways.

And so, hand in hand, my husband and I were left alone to stroll the streets of Paris. Moonlight, lamplight, lighted windows guided our steps towards a small, illuminated shooting gallery.

Who could resist?

Rifle in hand, my husband proceeded to demolish each moving target. Not bad for a novice but lucky marksman. The starry prize? A great ugly stonking toy bear, which my husband declined and chose instead a plastic rose.

He turned to me, smiled, brown eyes sought and found green eyes as he offered me this rose, "To the prettiest lady in Paris".

Again he smiled, this time a forever smile. At these touching words, I felt an unsummoned tear trickle down my cheek which was gently kissed away and I too was now smiling, smiling that same forever smile.

This precious rose, now brittle, I still have, still treasure.

From time to time, I remove it from its wrappings, I touch its petals, and I remember.

Once more I am smiling that forever smile as I recollect those tender words, that magic moment when I was the "Prettiest lady in Paris".

Whatever became of that "Prettiest Lady in Paris?" She grew old, that's what happened, garnering a plethora of wrinkles as she aged. "The song of the prune" became her serenade.

Now she lives with some old woman who has taken up residence in her mirror and who mimics her every move – We have become two old friends sat on a bench like two book ends.

A far cry from those heady days of youth so long ago.

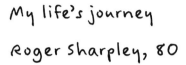
My life's journey
Roger Sharpley, 80

Lying awake in bed this morning at around 6am I was ruminating and reflecting on our visit yesterday to Jan's in Ringwood, and realising that what I was feeling was the trauma and extreme discomfort that I felt when I was at boarding school at the age of two and a half years old.

I had the feeling of complete and total helplessness and the sensation of utter despair, feeling totally trapped and powerless and unable to do anything to help what felt like a sense of incarceration. Being unable to help or protect myself in any way at all. It felt like 'a fate worse than death'.

This ruminating also enabled me, or led me to realise, that even now, today that I'm still aware, and continuing to have or hold these feelings or past beliefs that I'm still incapable of doing or discovering anything I can do even now to help myself in the way of my daily life, and therefore having to rely on other people as I did in the past, i.e. Sabine and therapy to come up with answers or knowledge of what it is I need to do in my life, in order to be able to help myself, actually carry on (and survive)!

Although, and despite an earlier period in my life, in my early 20s (22 years old) I was more than capable, (1967) of leaving home with a friend and going to live in Spain for the summer months, and then not wanting to return home to Bournemouth but live in London, again for a few months, before joining a 'Seismic Survey company' (for a period of over 16 years).

My first job for this company was working in Ethiopia on a boat in the Red Sea and then travelling down to Somalia, and on down the coast of Africa and to The Middle East. Then later to Scandinavia, Norway, The North Sea, Australia, Tasmania and New Zealand, the seismic boat that I was on was caught in a Hurricane, when we were in New Zealand, and it seemed like nobody on the 'boat' including myself thought we were going to survive!

What that experience brought up for me, was that I realised that I had actually had this feeling before, that I wasn't going to survive, and that was when I was sent to boarding school, and due to my failing health while I was there, the school recommended that I be returned home which was, I'm sure what enabled me to survive.

I think I was then able to discover for myself, over a period of time, what I had always wanted and needed at that very early stage in my life of two and a half years old, when I was 'abandoned' that LOVE and all the JOY and SECURITY that it can bring was always what I needed and longed for, and in order to discover this, I had to travel around the world, and as far away from my home as I could possibly get, to discover what it was I really longed for and was in need of, LOVE and BELONGING which I feel I have now finally found!

So now I would like to continue my life and discover each day for the rest of my life what I'm really grateful for.

AND

To achieve the happiness that can only come by changing how I feel in my inner self, and acknowledging the changes I've made in my life's journey, to help and support others, that I felt I was able to do, by becoming a Homeopath which I did for a period of about 37 years, thus coming full circle in my life to discovering what I truly am, through the love and compassion I found on my way!

Trucking Along

A Perera

The first crew were early, clangy, a bit. She had hair in many colours, excellently applied make up, gold eye shadow, and muscles, evidently, though her small frame didn't flaunt them. The others all men, looking as you'd expect them to. Possibly. They moved fast, blink twice and they'd be gone, like something there, then not, leaving the bins strewn, but close enough. Close enough for government work.

The second lot came later and argued with next door about fees and tops. Fees and tops. The quiet man, most aggrieved, insisted they'd broken his garden bin and he wanted a new one, this after they said he didn't pay the fee, or was it before? Odd to think of him arguing at all, the crew seemed nice enough to me, but they had their standards, and Alan had fallen outside those standards. One has to accept standards. At some point, all again peace.

Then there were longer delays. We peeked out, had they gone yet? No, still they stood, green and blue, plastic, closed, bulging.

When would the men come? It was all men again. We suspected different groups, perhaps different routes. Those of us with plastic bins envied the big house with its line of short, round tin bins standing on the path along the hedge, less bin, more nostalgia, waiting for the men to bring them out and put them back. Our bins, us in the smaller houses, got dropped on the 'sidewalk' as the American couple said, approximately where we lived. Perhaps Alan had a point about them breaking his lid.

A big move. The bins would no longer wait a day or even two at a bank holiday. They would be taken on the 'normal' day. Once a week, as usual. Once a fortnight, as usual for the garden bin. Alan offered me use of his garden bin, but I didn't think he meant it, so I didn't take him up on it. I recall the offer of apples. Take anything you can reach, he said. So I did; he wasn't happy. So I left them. Half of them went out in the garden bin, with the cutted up branches. My grammar, his grandson.

They brought him a new garden bin, with a good lid, the week after he died. Better than that, they brought him two. I'm not sure what he would have said, I think he would have rung and complained. He had the number on speed dial.

Then came the man who'd broken his foot. He was the advance guard, tossing paper from the paper container into the giant bin he hauled along, at speed. At speed both the tossing, and the hauling. I'd broken my foot too, we had short commiseration conversations at six am. He never stopped moving, he had to take his giant bin to the end of the road to rendezvous with the truck. His foot is better now, he's just as fast.

The garden bin is earlier. I have to be up to get it out. There are a few of us early up, I am a mess, the lady at the end of the road appears 'photographed for Vogue' in full length pink with three quarter sleaves. It's a nice dressing gown.

The family across the road have gone from one to three garden bins. Never over-filled, neatly lined up, an obedient line of three, lids closed. Alan would have thought something. Even I think something, but I don't know what it is I think. I probably wonder what's in those bins, there is only so much chopping one can do.

We have gone from team to team, argument to peace, bins to bins. We began with the early team and make-up at dawn, to later teams, back to an early team. We have said goodbye to Alan, and to Michael, children had left, babies have grown. Bin day remains, same time next week.

I outgrew old age
Simon Shelly

I became too old for sport – but then I outgrew being too old!

So this is my story of 'a memorable moment, event or day'. It's a bit of all three, but to get to it all, we have to go back in time. A very long way back in time. Bear with me.

When I was young, I really enjoyed sport. I wasn't a great player, nor did I have a range of sports on offer at my senior school: just the classic football, cricket (not good enough) and rugby (not big or aggressive enough).

When I left school, I carried on playing cricket – still not very well - but was at a loss what to do to keep fit in winter. Towards the end of yet another summer of modest cricket (non)achievement, one of my teammates had a sarcastic brainwave. Little did he know the full impact of what he was saying, or where it would end up.

His words to me were "You're not a very good wicketkeeper. You stop everything alright, but you can't catch. Why don't you try goalkeeping at hockey?" It was said in jest but the thought planted a seed.

That autumn I gave it a go and, wow! I had found my true sporting love. In no time I had got my head around the finer points of the rules and began to be able to work out where my goalposts were behind me, I loved it. A fiddly little ball which was a beast to try to hit – so kick it instead. I kicked it. A hard little ball which hurts like hell if it hits you – so wear protective gear. I wore protective gear. I had no fear of the ball and – glory be! – wasn't allowed to catch it, let alone try!

Time passed and, after a few seasons in the UK, work saw me live and work abroad. On the second of these assignments, I found myself in Paris. To my surprise, I found a small but passionate hockey community there and a vibrant league scene. So I spent the best part of three seasons keeping goal for a club just outside Paris, learning the dark arts of more than one nation's approach to the game.

Shortly after that, I discovered the bane of players immemorial: parenthood. The demands of having young kids were not compatible with disappearing for hours every Saturday afternoon. Then the kids grow up and you have a bit more time on your hands once again. Returning to hockey in your mid to late 40s, however, having last played it in your late 30s, is a cruel awakening to mortality. Didn't I used to be quicker? Did it always ache so much the day after a game? Did opponents run that fast before?

It doesn't get better. As forties give way to fifties, league hockey becomes ever tougher. The goals seem to fly in more regularly and you seem to be just a bit slow to make those saves you used to make without thinking. There must be something else?

Then I discovered there is something else. I bade farewell to Open Hockey – league hockey for all ages – and gave in to the inevitable. But not in a bad way. Into my life came the new horizons of veterans hockey, the wonderfully named Masters and even Grand Masters hockey. (Side note: am I alone in finding 'Grand Master' a bit dodgy – sort of Harry Potter meets Ku Klux Klan? Never mind, maybe it's just me).

There is a lively hockey scene for players much older than those you would find still playing most other team sports. I discovered the joys of hockey all over again. Farewell chasing after far younger players who are much too fast for you, hello a slightly slower very tactical game played by grizzly old seasoned players who still have great skill and hit the ball as hard as ever.

And so – at last - to my 'memorable moment, event and day'.

For the first time this past summer, I progressed from club to regional, representative hockey. One weekend in June, I proudly donned the goalkeeping smock of the London Over 65s as we did battle over two days and seven games with the other seven regions of England Hockey in our age group for the national title. I loved every minute of it and hope for more of the same in future.

The young wicketkeeper who couldn't catch now is the old hockey goalkeeper looking to play at the highest representative level he can. There are national hockey teams and international tournaments not just at Over 65 level, but more senior age groups than that. Who knows? Why not.

I used to be too old – but then I outgrew it!

They Walk Among Us
Tim Gilby, 63

Angela Rippon's Choice Award

Television documentaries and their presenters have a lot to answer for and principally Joanna Lumley in this particular case.

Spurred on by watching a travel show, in 2019 I was on holiday with my wife loosely following in the footsteps of Joanna Lumley on one of her trips to Japan. This woman has cost me a lot of money.

We had seen many of the major sites and cities of Honshu including the iconic dome at Hiroshima that had been at the epicentre of the atomic bomb. Later that day we travelled a few miles just along the coast to spend a few nights nearby on the picturesque island of Miyajima.

Towards the end of the next day after a walk to the nearby peak and having been mugged for our snacks by the tame deer that roam the island, we decided to hunt down a cup of coffee. Rather than stay on the main tourist drag along the waterfront, we decided to head a few streets inland in order to experience the locality. We came across a dimly lit shop that on the face of it looked like a second-hand curios and bookshop. It had a sign that said "coffee" however, so we headed in.

We were met by an elderly, grey and genteel lady who kept the shop. She identified that we were from the UK when we asked for coffee and cake. In her broken English explained that she only had Chiffon cake as it was the only cake that she could cook. But cake is cake in any language so that was fine by me.

As we enjoyed our refreshments the lady reappeared but this time carrying an English Japanese dictionary, the size of which would put many Church Bibles to shame. We emphasised that she did not need to apologise for her English, as we only knew three words in Japanese - hello, goodbye and thank you, but we could get by with that.

It was as we continued to chat with the aid of the dictionary that the old lady literally dropped the bombshell. She explained that she was a survivor of the Hiroshima atomic blast in 1945 when she was just two years old.

At rare moments like these it is difficult to quite take in the enormity of the message and I don't quite remember how I reacted. However, I do remember us continuing to chat for a while and being introduced to her son before we eventually hugged, said goodbye and went on her way.

I found it hard to get over, I'm not really sure that I have even now.

It did remind me of two other related meetings.

During my professional life I was required to hold a valid first aid qualification, so one day I was in the British Red Cross hall in Redhill practicing my bandaging on other trainees. I was asked to do a fist and hand bandage on another guy a good few years older than me. As I rolled up his cuff to begin I was taken aback. I saw a serial number tattooed on his skin. I immediately recognised it as a mark from a Nazi concentration camp. Nothing was said, nothing needed to be said.

I also recalled the time I spent at adult education evening classes learning German. Our teacher, a native German speaker, was a lovely lady named Sigi. As time went on and we got to know her better she revealed that she had come to the UK from Vienna, just before the start of World War Two. She had been one of the Kinder Transport children rescuees from the onset of war brought into the protection of the UK. They are commemorated in a statue outside Liverpool Street Station in the City of London.

I don't know if the people I speak of are still alive and even if they are, their generation will be diminishing in number all the time. That is why I feel that it is important to share these stories, not as people who witnessed the history but people who actually lived the history and are testament to those of future generations who cast doubt on past events.

As a trio they succinctly illuminate the course of World War Two and in the case of Sigi and the Japanese lady they neatly bookend the whole package.

I am not going to make any moral points, other than to say when reviewing history or especially the plight of some people in our modern world, there are plenty of lessons to be considered and learnt from these peoples' experiences.

It was a true honour to have met them. They walk among us.

Three Months in 1969
Mark Brody, 82

After three years in Zambia, and having got far from home, I wanted to have a little adventure. The Mini I had bought there had another petrol tank for long journeys and the rear seat was replaced by a locked box.

My first objective was to climb Kilimanjaro in Tanzania which was very exciting, and I climbed up to the top. It was very cold and very difficult. Unfortunately, today that is not the case due to climate change. On arriving at the very top I had to rest for some time. After recovering, going down was very easy. And a great relief!

My Mini & I sailed to India via the Seychelles. We docked in Mumbai. I retrieved the car and drove north. I saw the Taj Mahal and many other sites. At one I met a woman and asked her if she wanted a guide, meaning I'd share one with her to reduce the cost per person. Looking at my overgrown beard she replied, "No thank you!" Once I rented a room but, after finding mice running over me, I paid a little extra somewhere else.

I then drove into Pakistan, and I have a vague memory of filling up the petrol tank with aviation fuel! From Peshawar in Pakistan, I drove through the Khyber Pass to Kabul in Afghanistan. The boarding house (hardly a hotel) had many rooms, 6 metal beds in each, both sexes together. One thing that initially puzzled me was why no one got up at all early. I think they were stoned on hashish! It was very pleasant sightseeing in the early morning.

I met a group of roughish young men in Kabul. Two were ex-offenders. They had been going to India but were refused entry. We teamed up to go back to the UK together. We intended to drive in stages from Kabul to Kandahar, thence to Herat. However, their Volkswagen broke down and two of them hitched a ride to Kabul for spare parts. People stopped to give us water. In fact, we had set up a signboard to alert them to our need. Shortly, the lads returned with the necessary parts. All was well and we drove to Herat. The next stage home was driving westwards through Iran. The quickest route was on a very rough pot-holed road. The Mini did not have sufficient clearance for that road. One lad volunteered to come with me. I was delighted. We simply kept going west: Iran, Turkey, Bulgaria, and Yugoslavia.

I remember the joy of seeing pretty girls with miniskirts – a joy after the covered faces in Iran. It was a simple matter to drive through Austria, Germany, France, then across the channel HOME! The customs officer asked me what I had to declare I said "nothing". "What about the car?!" I'd forgotten that I'd bought it in Zambia. He didn't charge me though. The car was on its last wheels! It was a short drive to my Mother's house.

Shark

Grahame Money, 82

The end of our last year at boarding school in Sydney, in 1958, was anomalous. The lower years still had lessons and end of year exams, but we had already finished the state Leaving Certificate Exams and had no more lessons. What on earth were we doing still boarding at school.

I therefore suggested to three friends, and it was agreed, that we have a hitch-hiking race from Sydney to Surfers Paradise in Queensland, 400 miles or so. Pedro and I would be one team and Roger and Johnny the other.

For some reason, I felt that we needed provisions so I half-filled a duffle bag with cans of food to sustain us. I soon realised that one can, in fact, buy food all over Australia.

One beautiful summer morning, without telling the school, we walked out and made our way by local train to the northern outskirts of the city to try our luck hitchhiking and not without success. I recall sitting on top of a fully loaded truck, in the warm morning sun, as we made our way besides the Hawksebury River towards Gosford. Life seemed wonderful.

North from Sydney one can take the "high road", The New England Highway, or the "low road", The Pacific Highway to travel to southern Queensland. We didn't choose, rather it depended upon the destination of those who gave us lifts. The result was that Pedro and I took the coast road and Roger and Johny the high road.

Sometimes we spent hours waiting for a lift, but we made progress. That first night, Pedro and I slept in the Ballina Showground, in banana growing country. It was still only 15 years after the end of the war, and we occasionally had lifts from returned soldiers who had interesting stories to tell.

Late on the second day we crossed into Queensland, my first time outside of New South Wales, and in the early summer evening we reached Surfers' Paradise. There, Pedro and I made ourselves comfortable for a night on the beach. We made friends with a mange old dog whom we christened "Fang" or more fully "Fang the Wonder Dog". The Wonder Dog proved a great help in reducing my stock of tinned food.

The next day the others arrived after their adventures in the New England Tablelands.

We took to the surf on our first full day together. We were all at home in the water and we swam about 200 yards from the life savers flags. About mid-day we left the water to find something to eat in town.

When we returned, we observed, from the beach head, a loan swimmer in the water where we had been earlier. Suddenly he was lifted out of the water and flung in the air like a rag doll. A huge black shadow could be seen in the wave. Vast amounts of blood escaped the victim and quickly spread out in the water and in the surf. The life savers didn't hesitate and made their way to the victim, but he was dead.

We subsequently learned that the victim was an immigrant from communist Poland, a "New Australian". It was a sad end to his attempt to better himself in the "Lucky Country".

Later, in the evening sun a school of dolphins frolicked in the water and rode the waves, oblivious to the earlier drama, they were having a grand old time.

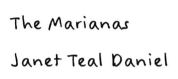

The Marianas
Janet Teal Daniel

'Janet, come quickly, I have a surprise for you.'

We were in the Cuartel Moncada, the Moncada Barracks in Santiago de Cuba, in the South of Cuba. It is the place where the revolution started. On July 26 1953, Fidel Castro and his band of revolutionaries stormed the barracks. The attack was unsuccessful, many were killed and those captured were tortured by the Regimental Intelligence Service, Fulgencio Batista's henchman. The Barracks is now a museum and also houses a school.

We were on holiday, a fortnight traveling on a Chinese bus with fourteen others visiting historical and cultural places of interest. Our guide, Lazarus, was very alive, an Ainsley Herriot look-a-like, the black TV chef, tall, smiley and wearing expensive foreign clothes that only those working in the tourist trade could possibly afford. He was well informed about the past and very willing to engage in discussions and debates about contemporary Cuba.

Most of the other travelers turned off and tuned into their MP3 players, but I couldn't get enough. I'd always dreamt of visiting Cuba. Che Guevara and Fidel Castro were my heroes in the 1960s. I spent a lot of time sitting by Lazarus at the front of the bus, asking him endless questions.

After a visit to Che Guevara's memorial, I asked Lazarus, "What about the women in Cuba's history and today? You haven't mentioned them. All I've seen so far are memorials to the men who fought and died in the revolution. Doesn't Communism profess to be egalitarian? Where is your women's history?'"

Lazarus looked embarrassed. He took a little time to answer and said defensively, "Wait and see."

A few days later we followed the disciples' trail through the Sierra Maestra, up to what had been Fidel and Che's secret mountain hideout, the place from where the revolution was masterminded. Lazarus handed us over to another guide, who gave us the spiel and then said, "I understand someone's interest in our women revolutionaries."I put up my hand and you could see the inner groan on the faces of the men, who just wanted to race to the top of the hill to see the site of the old radio station. The guide told us about a platoon of brave women, known as the 'Marianas,' named after the mother of a war hero, Mariana Grajales Cuello. They were women like Celia Sanchez, Fidel's right-hand woman, who was the architect and logician in the revolution, Haydee Santamaria and Melba Hernandez, who joined the assault on the Barracks, Vilma Espin and others, who formed the all-women platoon and engaged in active combat, fighting the enemy in harsh mountain conditions.

"Come on, quickly, here's my surprise!" Lazarus said the following day, ushering us into a side room in the Museum. Standing and waiting for us was a beautiful woman probably in her 60s with caramel skin, a shy expression, and a slight tremor that suggested she was suffering from Parkinson's Disease.

"She fought in the Revolution," he said, introducing us to the woman. "It's a wonderful coincidence. She just happened to be visiting the Museum today. She's brought some of her mementos for them to exhibit."

The woman opened her trembling hands and showed us a photograph of herself at aged 16 with her brother, both dressed as cadets. She had started like many others as a young teacher in the fight to irradicate illiteracy in rural Cuba. She showed us a piece of camouflage silk from a parachute and her war medals. There were so many questions I wanted to ask her, but where do you start with a female war hero? Her humble presence and complete lack of bravado moved us all. I noticed that I wasn't the only one with glistening eyes. At least two men in our party left the room finding the experience too emotional. Lazarus and the female war hero chatted for a bit longer. She gave her apologies-the Museum staff were waiting. She shook hands with each of us and spontaneously we all applauded her. She seemed embarrassed. "What were you chatting about?" I asked Lazarus as we left the building. "I was telling her how much we admired her generation and their commitment to the revolution." She said, "It's more difficult for your generation. At least we knew who the enemy was." "What was her name?" I asked.

"Oh... what was it? Oh dear, I've forgotten... Don't worry, the next time I visit the Barracks I'll find out. I'll email you. I promise."

That was over a decade ago. I never heard from Lazarus again. I often think of the unnamed Mariana and wonder if Lazarus will ever rise again.

Memories of
Wellington College

Richard Wellesley, 90

Richard Wellesley Benson 1948 — 1953

It was my first year and I was in the Lower Third. Douglas Young was my form master. I was the youngest and the smallest in the class. DY was an excellent form master, and he took the trouble to make his lessons interesting and varied as well as informative. He was a particularly good teacher of French, and we would often have to learn and recite French poetry. One day we came across a popular traditional French song 'Sur le Pont d'Avignon'. "Does anyone know the song?" he asked. Unwisely I put up my hand, "Come up here and sing it for us", he demanded. I sat on my hands. He repeated his demand. There was no way I was going to sing in my piping treble voice and make a fool of myself in front of the whole class, all of whom were bigger than me and many already had deep broken voices. There was a few moments of deathly hush. "Come and see me after the class", he said, and I knew what that usually meant.

After the class he gave me the surprisingly modest punishment of pumping up his bicycle tyres. I was still cross with him for embarrassing me so I decided to get my revenge by pumping up his tyres until they were on the point of bursting. The next day he told me one of his tyres had burst on the way home. He was nice enough to laugh the whole matter off. I did not confess — although I think he may have suspected that his burst tyre was exactly what I had intended.

In those days there was an Annual Lecture by some visiting literary celebrity. One year around 1949 the lecturer was Harold Nicolson. He was not a success. He seemed totally uninterested in his subject, mumbled through the whole script, and bored us all almost to tears. Our half-holiday had been ruined. It was with some dread that the next year we were told the visiting celebrity was to be a poet. What good was poetry to us when we could be practising in the nets, relaxing at Grubbies, or skiving off to the East Berks Golf Club? The poet was John Betjeman, and he knew exactly how to please a room full of sex-starved teenagers. Starting with 'Pot Pourri from a Surrey garden' extolling Pam 'you good big mountainous sports girl...the size of her thighs, the pout of her lips' running through half an hour of his poetry full of sexual innuendo, and ending with Joan Hunter-Dunn 'furnished and burnished by Aldershot sun', he held us entranced and amused. Rather to his astonishment at the close we gave him a standing ovation.

Beatings

I was caned on only three occasions. Two were for trivial offences and one was for a more serious offence. The first beating I had was by my housemaster Lewis. He was also my Biology teacher. I had failed to grasp some arcane and completely useless principle of biology. What thought process he went through to decide that a beating would help me to grasp this incomprehensible biological principle is hard to imagine. The second beating was for the equally trivial offence of leaving clothes about the changing room. I was pretty cross about both these canings, as I realised that they were both unfair and wrong. The third offence for which I was beaten was to desert the college rugby match a minute or two before the end in order to rush with a friend (Meadmore) to Grubbies to be first in the queue for ice creams. I richly deserved this beating as it was clearly right to cheer the College team at the end of the match. The Prefect who administered this punishment was Charles Huxtable — later General Sir Charles Huxtable. It was a very mild caning which he administered backhand in two casual strokes. Later in the changing room friends as ever came over to examine the bruises. Usually there were colourful weals to admire, but this time there was no mark at all, and my friends were not impressed. My friend and I should have felt happy about this mild caning, but instead we somehow felt cheated.

The Master — Harry House

I do indeed remember the Master, for whom we had great respect. Sadly, I never had any classes with him. I particularly remember his talk to the leavers on our last day at Wellington. He made two points that I clearly remember. The first was that it was very important to marry a woman that could share your interests, as well as being the object of your love. He said that he had been very fortunate in this way and he hoped we would be too. The second was that there was a link between alcohol and lust. 'Wine' he said — and I remember his exact words - "was made to make glad the heart of man" but it should not be abused, as it could lead you into trouble. His first injunction I rigorously followed, the second, along with most of my university friends, I did not.

Nina Simone- London
1986

Sarah Lavelle

Dr Russell Schechter's Choice Award ⭐

I remember how thrilled I felt when my boyfriend, Hugh, invited me to see Nina Simone at the legendary jazz club, Ronnie Scott's. We laugh about it now! About the fact that he was obviously trying to impress me. It evidently worked. We were married several years later.

In 1986, almost 40 years ago, I felt like the luckiest person alive. I was going to see the jazz legend, Nina Simone, in one of her last live performances in London. I didn't realise at the time how much of a coup it was to get to see 'The High Priestess of Soul" to perform at such an intimate club! She usually sang at much larger venues.

We took our time to get dressed. My boyfriend wore a silk navy suit, white shirt and Paul Smith designer tie and Cole Haan American loafers with a skirt and tassels. I wore an Alberta Ferretti black vintage cocktail dress, which I borrowed from a friend in the fashion business. My Manolo Blahnik designer shoes were purchased at the last minute. They were the highest heels I had ever worn and I had yet to master the art of walking in them. This was an important occasion and I wanted everything to be perfect.

We took a black cab to Ronnie Scott's, 47 Frith Street in Soho. As I stepped out onto the pavement, I slid my arm through Hugh's and teetered very slowly to the entrance. No way was I going to trip and fall and ruin what was going to be the perfect date. I remember asking myself why hadn't my mother ever given me lessons in walking in heels? Mind you I didn't ever re- member her wearing heels. She was a 'soap and water girl', a war time baby, who had no time for glamour, she was always too busy working! So instead, I focused on visualising myself parading down the red carpet like a movie star!

At the entrance, we could see photos and posters for all the jazz stars who had performed at the iconic club. Zoot Sims, Stan Getz, Ella Fitzgerald, Sarah Vaughan, Buddy Rich and Nina Si- mone. The most extraordinary jazz wall of fame.

The maître d' took us into the music room and to our table. It was to the right at the front of the stage. Hugh ordered a bot- tle of Mateus Rose. I took a large sip of wine and can remember thinking how cool it was to be drinking chilled rose from the unique shaped bottle and about to see Nina Simone.

Then, the Diva herself came on the stage wearing a strapless gown. She sat at the piano, waiting silently until the audience hushed and was ready. You could tell she instinctively knew when it was the right moment, she was known for it. Nina had to be poised and ready before hitting a note, starting her performance with Gershwin's "I Love You, Porgy".

The lights shone directly above her and she was hot…she wiped her dripping face more than once with a towel. As she sang, I was captivated by the magic and emotion that made her the star she still was and had been. Nina Simone was a child prodigy. She was a defiant woman, a young star during the Civil Rights movement and her songs tapped into her anger deep inside. However, in 1985 her performance seemed more personal than political. She sang a sad and moving song "For a While", a declaration of love after the love affair is over. "For five minutes the sun is shining and everything is beautiful. Then all of a sudden you realize that the person you cared about is gone, and it all comes back… one of those little holes in grief when it becomes even more painful."

Simone wrapped with "My Baby Just Cares for Me", a song that was on the original Bethlehem disk. As a result of a television commercial, it became a smash hit for her thirty years later in 1987 and reinvigorated her career.

I felt a deep sense of sadness and the pain of being a black American woman moulded by her race, her anger and her life. Even though I was white and born many years later in the UK, I could appreciate her talent but had yet to experience her sadness about the ending of a love affair. But what I did understand that her music was a gift from God and that her performance was not the easiest listen but it was definitely the most memorable live performance of my life.

I Offer This Keepsake to You

Lisa Jennings

I offer this keepsake to you.
Keep it with you
Keep it safely
So you can remember yourself
always with love.
When you have nothing
Or
Think you have nothing
Be careful to treasure yourself,
The way the sun treasures golden corn in summer.
The way hand knitted, woolen socks treasure your feet
In Winter.
Even if you have lost everything
Or
Think you have lost everything
Remember
To treasure yourself.
To embrace yourself.

To wrap yourself
In how much the world needs you.
In how hard it is just to get born.
Fill your belly with sunlight.
Treasure yourself
The way the sun
Treasures you.
Shine
Brightly.

ABOUT AGE UK RICHMOND

Age UK Richmond is a local independent charity fully dedicated to helping older people in the borough of Richmond upon Thames. Since its inception in 1965, it has helped thousands of local older people. Reducing loneliness and isolation, and improving health and wellbeing, are Age UK Richmond's guiding principles.

Age UK Richmond offer a range of preventative services to ensure that later years are fulfilling and enjoyable, and that older people can maintain connections within their communities.

As our population gets older, we will have to work harder and harder to meet the increasing demand for our services. Please donate to us if you can.

A donation to Age UK Richmond can be a lifeline, ensuring local older people can have someone to turn to.

To find out how you can donate please visit our website

www.ageukrichmond.org.uk

If you are thinking on leaving a lasting gift in your Will to Age UK Richmond, please kindly use these details:

Age UK Richmond upon Thames, Registered office:

The White House Community Centre, 45 The Avenue, Hampton, Richmond upon Thames, TW12 3RN.

Registered Charity No. 1084211.
Registered in England and Wales number 4116911.

ID111288 03/12